Past Examina
Suggested Solutions

Contract Law

LLB

University of London
External Examinations

HLT Publications

HLT PUBLICATIONS
200 Greyhound Road, London W14 9RY

Examination Questions
© The University of London 1985, 1986, 1987, 1988, 1989, 1990
Solutions © The HLT Group Ltd 1993

All HLT publications enjoy copyright protection and the copyright belongs to The HLT Group Ltd.

All rights reserved. No part of this publication may be reproduced or transmitted in any form or by any means, electronic, mechanical, photocopying, recording or otherwise, or stored in any retrieval system of any nature without either the written permission of the copyright holder, application for which should be made to The HLT Group Ltd, or a licence permitting restricted copying in the United Kingdom issued by the Copyright Licensing Agency.

Any person who infringes the above in relation to this publication may be liable to criminal prosecution and civil claims for damages.

ISBN 0 7510 0378 6

British Library Cataloguing-in-Publication.

A CIP Catalogue record for this book is available from the British Library.

Printed and bound in Great Britain.

CONTENTS

ACKNOWLEDGEMENT

The questions used are taken from past University of London LLB (External) Degree examination papers and our thanks are extended to the University of London for the kind permission which has been given to us to use and publish the questions.

Caveat:

The answers given are not approved or sanctioned by the University of London and are entirely our responsibility.

They are not intended as 'Model Answers', but rather as Suggested Solutions.

The answers have two fundamental purposes, namely:

1. To provide a detailed example of a suggested solution to examination questions, and
2. To assist students with their research into the subject and to further their understanding and appreciation of the subject of Laws.

Note:

Please note that the solutions in this book were written in the year of the examination for each paper. They were appropriate solutions at the time of preparation, but students must note that certain caselaw and statutes may subsequently have changed.

ACKNOWLEDGEMENT

[illegible] taken from past University [illegible] examination papers [illegible] which has [illegible]

[illegible]

[illegible]

[illegible]

[illegible]

N[illegible]

Please note that [illegible]

INTRODUCTION

Why choose HLT publications

Holborn College has earned an International reputation over the past ten years for the outstanding quality of its teaching, Textbooks, Casebooks and Suggested Solutions to past examination papers set by the various examining bodies.

Our expertise is reflected in the outstanding results achieved by our students in the examinations conducted by the University of London, the Law Society, the Council of Legal Education and the Associated Examining Board.

The object of Suggested Solutions

The Suggested Solutions have been prepared by College lecturers experienced in teaching to this specific syllabus and are intended to be an example of a full answer to the problems posed by the examiner.

They are not 'model answers', for at this level there almost certainly is not just one answer to a problem, nor are the answers written to strict examination time limits.

The opportunity has been taken, where appropriate, to develop themes, suggest alternatives and set out additional material to an extent not possible by the examinee in the examination room.

We feel that in writing full opinion answers to the questions that we can assist you with your research into the subject and can further your understanding and appreciation of the law.

Notes on examination technique

Although the SUBSTANCE and SLANT of the answer changes according to the subject-matter of the question, the examining body and syllabus concerned, the TECHNIQUE of answering examination questions does not change.

You will not pass an examination if you do not know the substance of a course. You may pass if you do not know how to go about answering a question although this is doubtful. To do well and to guarantee success, however, it is necessary to learn the technique of answering problems properly. The following is a guide to acquiring that technique.

Time

All examinations permit only a limited time for papers to be completed. All papers require you to answer a certain number of questions in that time, and the questions, with some exceptions carry equal marks.

It follows from this that you should never spend a disproportionate amount of time on any question. When you have used up the amount of time allowed for any one question STOP and go on to the next question after an abrupt conclusion, if necessary. If you feel that you are running out of time, then complete your answer in note form. A useful way of ensuring that you do not over-run is to write down on a piece of scrap paper the time at which you should be starting each part of the paper. This can be done in the few minutes before the examination begins and it will help you to calm any nerves you may have.

Reading the question

It will not be often that you will be able to answer every question on an examination paper. Inevitably, there will be some areas in which you feel better prepared than others. You will prefer to answer the questions which deal with those areas, but you will never know how good the questions are unless you read the whole examination paper.

You should spend at least 10 MINUTES at the beginning of the examination reading the questions. Preferably, you should read them more than once. As you go through each question, make a brief note on the examination paper of any relevant cases and/or statutes that occur to you even if you think you may not answer that question: you may well be grateful for this note towards the end of the examination when you are tired and your memory begins to fail.

Re-reading the answers

Ideally, you should allow time to re-read your answers. This is rarely a pleasant process, but will ensure that you do not make any silly mistakes such as leaving out a 'not' when the negative is vital.

The structure of the answer

Almost all examination problems raise more than one legal issue that you are required to deal with. Your answer should include the following:

Identify the issues raised by the question

This is of crucial importance and gives shape to the whole answer. It indicates to the examiner that you appreciate what he is asking you about.

This is at least as important as actually answering the questions of law raised by that issue.

The issues should be identified in the first paragraph of the answer.

Deal with those issues one by one as they arise in the course of the problem

This, of course, is the substance of the answer and where study and revision pays off.

If the answer to an issue turns on a provision of a statute, CITE that provision briefly, but do not quote it from any statute you may be permitted to bring into the examination hall.

Having cited the provision, show how it is relevant to the question.

If there is no statute, or the meaning of the statute has been interpreted by the courts, CITE the relevant cases

'Citing cases' does not mean writing down the nature of every case that happens to deal with the general topic with which you are concerned and then detailing all the facts you can think of.

You should cite only the most relevant cases – there may perhaps only be one. No more facts should be stated than are absolutely essential to establish the relevance of the case. If there is a relevant case, but you cannot remember its name, it is sufficient to refer to it as 'one decided case'.

Whenever a statute or case is cited, the title of statute or the name of the case should be underlined

This makes the examiner's job much easier because he can see at a glance whether the relevant material has been dealt with, and it will make him more disposed in your favour.

Having dealt with the relevant issues, summarise your conclusions in such a way that you answer the question

A question will often say at the end simply 'Advise A', or B, or C, etc. The advice will usually turn on the individual answers to a number of issues. The point made here is that the final paragraph should pull those individual answers together and actually give the advice required. For example, it may begin something like: 'The effect of the answer to the issues raised by this question is that one's advice to A is that ...'

Related to the previous paragraph, make sure at the end that you have answered the question

For example, if the question says 'Advise A', make sure that is what your answer does. If you are required to advise more than one party, make sure that you have dealt with all the parties that you are required to and no more.

Some general points

You should always try to get the examiner on your side. One method has already been mentioned – the underlining of case names, etc. There are also other ways as well.

Always write as neatly as you can. This is more easily done with ink than with a ball-point.

Avoid the use of violently coloured ink eg turquoise; this makes a paper difficult to read.

Space out your answers sensibly: leave a line between paragraphs. You can always get more paper. At the same time, try not to use so much paper that your answer book looks too formidable to mark. This is a question of personal judgment.

NEVER put in irrelevant material simply to show that you are clever. Irrelevance is not a virtue and time spent on it is time lost for other, relevant, answers.

UNIVERSITY OF LONDON
INTERMEDIATE EXAMINATION IN LAWS 1985
for External Students

ELEMENTS OF THE LAW OF CONTRACT

Friday, 21st June: 10.00 am to 1.00 pm

Answer *FIVE* questions of the following NINE questions.

1 Alan, a wholesaler, wrote to Ben and other retailers that he had just taken delivery of some high quality video tapes and was offering them for sale at £495 per hundred. On April 1 Ben sent a written order for two hundred tapes 'to be delivered by April 30' and asked Alan to send 'written confirmation as soon as possible'.

Ben heard nothing further from Alan and on April 22 he telephoned to find out whether Alan had received the order. Alan told him that everything was fine and that the confirmation would be on its way soon.

On the morning of May 2 Alan posted a confirmation of Ben's order, but during the afternoon he discovered that a number of the video tapes were defective and that he no longer had enough to satisfy all the orders which had been placed. He immediately sent a telex to Ben 'Cannot accept your order, as tapes sold out'. Ben received the written confirmation the next morning. No tapes have been delivered.

Advise Ben.

2 Colin made the following promise:

i) to give his daughter, Diana, £500 if she will abandon her career as a photographic model and become a social worker;

ii) to pay his secretary, Enid, £250 for having been willing to give up her lunch hour when necessary during the previous three months;

iii) to pay Fred, who has a contract with the local newsagent to deliver the newspapers in that area, £10 if he delivers the newspaper by 8 am every day for a month and puts it through a letter-box without tearing it;

iv) to give his old lawn-mower to George, a neighbour, if George collects it from the garden shed.

Advise Colin to what extent, if at all, the above promises are legally binding on him.

3 Henry, a bus conductor, makes furniture in his spare time. After seeing them advertised in a magazine, he ordered one of Ian's 'Handyman' portable work-benches. Soon afterwards Henry received a letter thanking him for the order and saying that delivery would be made 'subject to our usual conditions'. Two weeks later the workbench was delivered together with a sales note setting out Ian's 'Conditions of Sale'.

The first time Henry used it, the workbench collapsed. Henry fell and suffered serious injuries; an inflammable liquid he was using was spilled and a fire started which caused extensive damage to his house. Ian's Conditions of Sale state that all conditions and warranties are expressly excluded and that Ian is not to be liable for any loss or damage however caused.

Advise Henry. Would your answer be different if Henry sold the furniture he makes at a stall in the town's market?

4 Joanna owned a health food shop which she wished to sell. She was approached by Kate who was interested in buying the shop. Joanna told Kate that the demand for health foods would 'increase dramatically' as people became more health conscious and that since health foods were all 'natural' there was no risk of trouble from local authority health inspectors. Joanna also said that the shop made 'up to £1,000 profit a week'. She offered to show Kate the accounts, but Kate said she was happy to take Joanna's word for it.

After buying the shop for £50,000, Kate discovered that demand for health foods was falling and that in the previous two years the weekly profit had only once reached £1,000 and was generally below £200. The health inspector has also visited the premises and required her to stop selling certain items which infringe EEC regulations.

Advise Kate.

5 'A common mistake, even on a most fundamental matter, does not make a contract void at law: but it makes it voidable in equity.' (per Lord Denning MR in *Magee* v *Penine Insurance*).

Explain and comment.

6 Linda is seventeen years old and a first year student of fashion design. Believing it would help her with her studies she

enrolled for a series of lessons at a private modelling school at a fee of £200. She also purchased a de luxe sewing machine for £300 and, at the suggestion of her tutor Melvyn, bought 100 shares from Melvyn in a company run by Melvyn's wife, Norma, which manufactures handbags.

Linda has now given up the modelling lessons. She failed to pay the £200 and the school is demanding payment. Linda would also like to cancel the transactions concerning the sewing machine and the shares and have her money back.

Advise Linda.

7 'English law holds that no stranger to the consideration can take advantage of a contract, although it was made for his benefit'.

Explain and comment. To what extent do you consider that this statement presents an accurate picture of the legal position?

8 'Unless performance of the contract has become actually impossible, the fact that unforeseen events have made performance more burdensome is usually regarded as no more than one of life's misfortunes which the defendant has to bear.'

Discuss.

9 In January Olive, a successful business executive living and working in London, was appointed manager of a firm in Manchester, commencing on April 1, 1985. Having found a house she liked in Manchester, Olive engaged Paul, a builder, to do some renovation to it, the contract providing that the work would be completed by March 31 at the latest.

In breach of contract Paul did not complete the renovation until May 31st and Olive was unable to move into the house until June. During April and May Olive continued to live in London at the weekends, flying to Manchester and back each week, and stayed in a five star hotel in Manchester during the week. She also engaged a nanny to look after her two small children during her absence.

Olive is now claiming that Paul should pay her air fares between London and Manchester, the hotel bills, the cost of the nanny and a 'substantial sum' to compensate her for the emotional distress of being separated from her family.

Advise Paul.

QUESTION 1

Suggested Solution

In advising Ben one must consider whether a contract for the sale of video tapes was concluded between him and Alan in the course of the various communications passing between them; if it was, then Ben will have an action for damages against Alan for non-delivery.

The first communication was Alan's letter to Ben 'offering' tapes for sale at £495 per hundred. On the facts there seems no reason for not attributing to the letter the ordinary meaning of the language used, namely that it is a contractual offer and not merely an invitation to treat. Whilst it is true that the test is one of substance rather than form, and it is possible for a document termed 'offer' to be only an invitation to treat (*Spencer* v *Harding* (1)) there is nothing in Alan's letter which might lead a court to conclude that it was not intended to have contractual force.

Ben's response was a written order dated 1st April. As a matter of construction this must be regarded as a counter-offer because it seeks to introduce a new term: *Butler Machine Tool Co Ltd* v *Ex-cell-o Corp* (2). The new term is for delivery by 30 April, Alan's letter having been wholly silent as to delivery dates. Further, it is clear that Ben so regarded it, because he asked for Alan's 'written confirmation': in law, Ben was prescribing the mode of acceptance of his counter-offer, *Manchester Diocesan Council for Education* v *Commercial & General Investments Ltd* (3). Also, by requiring delivery by 30 April, Ben is clearly stipulating that Alan must accept his counter-offer within that time scale.

The next communication is the telephone conversation on 22 April. The difficulty here is to determine whether what Alan said amounted to an acceptance of Ben's counter-offer. On balance it was likely that a court would conclude that the language used was too ambiguous on both sides. Ben did not clearly dispense with the requirement of written confirmation (ie. acceptance) and Alan did not unequivocably commit himself to honour Ben's order. It is clear that both parties regarded the counter-offer as open for acceptance, but that there had not, at that time, been an acceptance in the prescribed form from Alan.

On the other hand it is possible that the telephone conversation was not wholly devoid of legal effect. It is possible to construe it as being an indication by Ben that his counter-offer is still open for acceptance by Alan, and moreover, that by not making any reference to the 30 April delivery date, Ben impliedly waived that date or, alternatively, thereby extended the duration of his offer. A not dissimilar situation arose in the *Manchester Diocesan Council* case in which Buckley J held that by implication an offer remained open for acceptance where the offeree had manifested an intention to accept without having done so in law.

Thus by 2 May Ben's counter-offer was still open to Alan to accept and had not lapsed on 30 April. By posting his confirmation on the morning of 2 May, in English law Alan will be considered at the moment to have accepted it. This is the effect of the so-called postal acceptance rule, originally laid down in *Adams* v *Lindsell* (4) and affirmed numerous times subsequently, eg *Household Fire Insurance Co Ltd* v *Grant* (5), *Henthorn* v *Fraser* (6), *Holwell Securities Ltd* v *Hughes* (7) and, most recently by the House of Lords, obiter, in *Brinkibon Ltd* v *Stahag Stahl* (8).

The rule will normally apply where it is reasonable for the offeree to accept by post, where the letter of acceptance is properly stamped and addressed and where the offeror has not otherwise stipulated. Whereas the first two conditions are satisfied here, it is at least possible that Ben has, possibly by inadvertence, excluded the operation of the rule by his request for 'written confirmation'. Conversely one could argue that all Ben was thereby requesting was an acceptance in writing, not that it was only to be effective when received by him, and certainly the language is much less clear than that used in *Holwell* where the offeror required 'notice in writing' of the offeree's acceptance.

If Ben's counter-offer is regarded as having excluded the postal acceptance rule, no contract is formed because Alan's subsequent rejection by telex overtakes and arrived before his letter. Conversely if the rule is regarded as applying, the effect of the telex is less certain. Then one is faced with the difficulty which has yet to be resolved in the courts, namely whether the offeree can withdraw a posted letter of acceptance by means of a speedier mode of communication which overtakes the letter.

An orthodox application of the postal rule would demand the answer 'no'. Ordinarily, once an acceptance is effective the offeree has no right unilaterally to retire from it, and it would seem unjust that the offeror should be bound once the letter is posted, yet the offeree retain the right to withdraw at any time before receipt of the letter by the offeror. In two Commonwealth cases, *Wenkheim* v

Arndt (9) (New Zealand) and *A to Z Bazaars* v *Minister of Agriculture* (10) (South Africa) the courts refused to allow withdrawal though without considering in detail the policy reasons one way or the other, and textbook writers too generally oppose allowing withdrawal, eg Cheshire and Fifoot and Treitel.

The most vehement proponent of the argument in favour of withdrawal is Professor Hudson (11). He argues that the postal rule is one of convenience not logic and ought not to be inflexibly applied. He says that the offeror is not prejudiced by allowing the offeree to withdraw, since until he receives the letter, he is unaware of the 'acceptance'; that the offeror should be considered to take the risk of withdrawal, as he takes the risk of the letter being lost or delayed (*Grant*'s case); and that it is open to the offeror to protect himself against withdrawal by framing his offer appropriately. Further, in *Dick* v *US* (12) an American court held a withdrawal to be effective, though the authority of the case is somewhat diminished by the fact that the state in question allowed posted letters to be retrieved by the sender (unlike England).

Whilst Professor Hudson's arguments are cogent and persuasive, it is submitted that the English courts would decide against allowing withdrawal, following their brethren in *Wenkheim* and *A to Z Bazaars*, and hold that Alan is bound by his letter and that his subsequent telex is of no effect in law. On this footing, Ben would have a claim for damages against Alan for his failure to deliver the tapes.

References

1) (1870) LR 5 CP 561
2) [1979] 1 WLR 401
3) [1970] 1 WLR 242
4) (1818) 1 B & Ald 681
5) (1879) 4 Ex D 216
6) [1892] 2 Ch 27
7) [1974] 1 WLR 155
8) [1983] 2 AC 24
9) (NZ) 1 JR (1873)
10) [1974] 4 SA 392 (c)
11) (1966) 82 LQR 167
12) 82 F Supp 326 (1949)

QUESTION 2

Suggested Solution

i) If Diana does become a social worker, then prima facie Colin is bound by his promise: he has made an offer to her, and by abandoning her career as a model she both accepts the offer and furnishes consideration. However, Colin may be able to avoid liability if he can persuade the court that there was no intention to create legal relations.

The traditional approach of the courts to 'family' agreements of this nature is that there is rebuttable presumption that the parties did not intend to create legal relations: *Balfour* v *Balfour* (1). It is perfectly possible for a parent and child to enter into a binding contract, but there must be clear evidence that they intended legal consequences to flow from their agreement. Thus in *Jones* v *Padavatton* (2) the majority of the Court of Appeal held that a mother's promise to her daughter to pay her a monthly allowance if she moved from the United States to England and read for the bar was held to be unenforceable. At first sight, *Jones* would appear to be close to the present case. However, one point of distinction is that in *Jones* the court was heavily influenced by the vagueness of the agreement; here, by contrast, the agreement is precise and specific.

Although this distinction of fact does exist, ultimately it would be likely that the court would hold on these facts, in the context of a parent-child relationship the presumption had not been rebutted and that Colin was under no liability to Diana.

ii) Colin's promise to Enid is in return for her having given up her lunch hour in the previous three months: this immediately raises the problem of past consideration.

Because consideration is given in return for the promisor's promise and, once furnished, the promise becomes binding and irrevocable, acts done prior to the making of the promise cannot constitute good consideration. Past consideration, so it is said, is no consideration: *Roscorla* v *Thomas* (3) and *Re McArdle* (4). A simple application of this rule would mean that Enid had no claim against Colin.

The rule is, however, subject to a number of acceptions. The relevant one here derives from the decisions in *Lampleigh* v *Brathwait* (5), *Kennedy* v *Brown* (6) and *Re Casey's Patents* (7), and was recently affirmed and restated in *Pao On* v *Lau Yiu* (8). The exception provides that an antecedent act can be good consideration for a subsequent promise where (a) it was done at the promisor's request, (b) it was understood that the act was to be remunerated by payment or the conferment of some other benefit and (c) the payment or benefit, if promised in advance, would have been legally enforceable.

Accordingly, if Enid can satisfy these three conditions, Colin will be liable on his promise. If she cannot, and merely gave up her lunch hour in the hope, rather than the legal expectation, of payment, Colin is not liable. On the limited facts given it is impossible to reach a conclusion one way or the other.

iii) Fred is already bound by his contract with the newsagent to deliver newspapers: the issue raised is whether by delivering the paper by 8.00 am and not tearing it, he furnishes consideration for Colin's promise. It is submitted that Fred does furnish consideration in one of two ways. First, unless his contract with the newsagent obliges him to deliver Colin's paper by 8.00 am, in doing so he is doing over and above his existing contractual duty: *Hartley* v *Ponsonby* (9). The same cannot be said about not tearing the paper since this must clearly be an implied if not an express term of his contract with the newsagent.

Secondly, and more simply, as the law stands it matters not whether Fred is doing more than he is bound to do by his contract with the newsagent, or whether he is merely performing his existing contractual obligation. A succession of cases in the nineteenth century, namely *Shadwell* v *Shadwell* (10), *Scotson* v *Pegg* (11) and *Chichester* v *Cobb* (12), affirmed and followed recently in *New Zealand Shipping Co Ltd* v *AM Saterthwaite and Co Ltd* (13) and *Pao On* v *Lau Yin* established that the performance of an existing contractual duty owed to a third party (as opposed to the promisor) is good consideration. It therefore follows that Fred does furnish consideration for Colin's promise and the latter is bound to honour it.

iv) It is submitted that this instance illustrates the distinction between consideration and a condition. No contract exists between Colin and George because no consideration moves from the latter to support the former's promise. The true legal analysis is that Colin is promising to make a gift of the lawn-mower to George providing the latter collects it, it is a conditional gift: *Wyatt* v *Kreglinger* (14). At any time before George collects, Colin is at liberty to revoke his promise; once George has collected, the conditional gift becomes unconditional and complete and property in the lawn-mower will pass to George.

References

1) [1919] 2 KB 571
2) [1969] 1 WLR 328
3) (1842) 3 QB 234
4) [1951] Ch 669
5) (1615) Hob 105
6) (1863) 13 CBNS
7) [1892] 1 Ch 104
8) [1980] AC 614
9) (1857) 7 E & B 872
10) (1860) 9 CB (NS) 159
11) (1861) 6 H & N 295
12) (1866) 14 LT 433
13) [1975] AC 154
14) [1933] 1 KB 793

QUESTION 3

Suggested Solution

In advising Henry as to his rights against Ian, one must consider the effect, if any, in law of the exclusion clause contained in the 'Conditions of Sale' on Ian's sale note. Ordinarily one would consider first whether the clause was incorporated as a term of the contract between Ian and Henry and, secondly, if it was, whether on its true construction it applies to the breach of contract which has occurred, before proceeding to examine the possible application of the Unfair Contract Terms Act 1977. On the unusual facts of this case, it is submitted that the 1977 Act disposes of the matter entirely, for reasons which will be explained.

Assuming, against Henry, that the clause was incorporated and on its true construction did apply to protect Ian, one must then consider the 1977 Act. The Act applies to this contract because the liability sought to be excluded by Ian is business liability: s1(3) thereof. Further, the contract is one for the sale of goods into which certain conditions are implied by ss13 and 14 of the Sale of Goods Act 1979, namely that the goods should correspond with their contractual description, be of merchantable quality and be reasonably fit for the purpose for which the goods are bought. It is submitted that Ian is in clear breach of s14(2) and (3) of the 1979 Act, and probably s13(1) as well, because the workbench collapsed the first time Henry used it. Such a product cannot possibly be said either to be of merchantable quality or reasonably fit for the purpose for which it was intended. Henry therefore has a good claim for damages for breach of these implied conditions.

The exclusion of restriction of liability for breach of inter alia ss13 and 14 of the 1979 Act is controlled by s6 of the 1977 Act. Section 6 (2) renders clauses excluding or restricting such liability totally ineffective as against a person 'dealing as consumer'. This expression is defined in s12 of the 1977 Act and, in the present case, sub-paragraphs (a)–(c) of s12(1) must be satisfied, namely that:

a) Henry did not make the contract in the course of a business nor held himself out as doing so;

b) Ian did make the contract in the course of a business;

c) the goods were of a type ordinarily supplied for private use or consumption.

The only doubt can arise in relation to (c). It is submitted that workbenches are goods which are ordinarily supplied for private use or consumption: 'do-it-yourself' is a common hobby and workbenches are frequently purchased by such persons. Further, it is likely that the court would construe the word 'ordinarily' as meaning 'commonly', rather than 'on the majority of occasions'; the 1977 Act is a protective statute which would be given a generous rather than a narrow construction, and in any event under s12(3) the burden of proof would be on Ian to show that Henry did not deal as consumer. One's advice to Henry would be that Ian would be unable to do so and, accordingly, Henry has an unanswerable claim for damages in respect of all heads of loss suffered by him.

On the alternative footing that Henry sells the furniture at a market stall different considerations arise and now one must discuss first, the possible incorporation of the clause and, secondly, its construction, before examining again the 1977 Act.

As to incorporation, it is vital to pinpoint the precise moment at which the contract is concluded. The machinery of formation is that Ian's advertisement in the magazine is an invitation to treat only, *Partridge* v *Crittenden* (1). Henry's 'order' is a contractual offer, which Ian can accept or reject. By replying in the terms in which he did, Ian did not accept Henry's offer but himself made a counter-offer because his letter introduced new terms into the proposed transaction; namely his standard conditions of business, *Butler Machine Tool Co Ltd* v *Ex-cell-o Corp* (2).

Although Ian does not expressly accept that counter-offer, in law he will be considered to have done so when the workbench was delivered to him together with a copy of Ian's conditions, and he accepted and used the bench: *Brogden* v *Metropolitan Railway* (3). Moreover, providing the copy of Ian's terms were delivered to Henry in such a way as to give him reasonable notice of their contents, including the exclusion clause, Henry will be bound by them: *Parker* v *SE Railway* (4).

In conclusion, on incorporation, whilst the position is not open and shut, it is very likely that the court will regard Ian's terms as forming a part of the contract between him and Henry.

The question of construction can be dealt with very shortly. Ian's exclusion clause is in blanket form and, as such, applies at common law to protect him from liability. A similar clause was upheld in *L'Estrange* v *Graucob Ltd* (5) and since *Photo Production Ltd* v *Securicor Transport Ltd* (6) and *George Mitchell Ltd* v *Finney Lock Seeds Ltd* (7) it is settled law that there is a category of fundamental breaches or of fundamental terms, liability for which can never be excluded. Moreover, even if liability in negligence can be established against Ian, the words loss of damage 'however caused' were held in *Joseph Travers & Sons Ltd* v *Cooper* (8) to exclude liability for negligence. Thus on the true construction of the clause, Ian is protected.

Thus one turns to the 1977 Act again. On this alternative footing Ian will be able to establish that Henry was not dealing as consumer as defined in s12(1) because Henry bought the workbench for use in his business selling furniture at the market. The prohibition on excluding liability for breach of ss13 and 14 of the 1979 Act imposed by s6(2) of the 1977 Act therefore does not apply; instead s6(3) applies, and the clause will only be effective insofar as it satisfies the requirement of reasonableness set out in s11(1) of the 1977 Act.

Before moving to s11(1) one should observe in passing that if Ian was guilty of negligence in the construction of the workbench, then s2 of the 1977 Act will apply to Henry's claim in tort. As to Henry's claim in respect of personal injuries, s2(1) would operate to render Ian's clause totally ineffective; in respect of the damage to the house s2(2) would once more subject the clause to the reasonableness test laid down in s11(1). Since there is no evidence one way or the other on negligence this point will not be pursued further.

The requirement of reasonableness is defined in s11(1) as being that the term shall have been a fair and reasonable one to be included having regard to the circumstances which were, or ought reasonably to have been, known to or in the contemplation of the parties when the contract was made. The language of the sub-section is unequivocal: the enquiry is whether it was reasonable to include this clause in this contract, not whether it is reasonable to permit reliance on it.

The burden of proof is on Ian to persuade the court that the clause does satisfy the requirement of reasonableness, s11(5), and s11(2) further informs the court, in this case, to have regard to the guidelines specified in Schedule 2 to the Act in considering whether or not the clause is reasonable. The material guidelines here are (a), (c) and (e) of Schedule 2: (in short) the parties' respective bargaining strengths, Henry's knowledge or ignorance of the clause and whether it is a common one in the trade, and the fact that the workbench was a standard item and not a 'special order' from Henry.

In addition, *R W Green Ltd* v *Cade Bros Farms* (9) and the *George Mitchell* case (decided under s55(4) of the Sale of Goods Act 1893, as amended, but still of assistance), indicate that the courts will also look at matters such as the availability of insurance to both parties, the size of their respective commercial concerns, and the scope of the clause eg does it exclude all liability, including negligence, or merely certain types, or perhaps only restrict rather than exclude it altogether.

Advising on reasonableness under the 1977 Act is not an exact science. As Lord Bridge said in the *George Mitchell* case, what may appear reasonable to one judge may seem unreasonable to another, yet both decisions may be the result of the proper exercise of judicial discretion. As a matter of judgment, it is submitted that Ian's clause would not satisfy the requirement of reasonableness for the following reasons:

i) it is not referred to either in the magazine advertisement, or in the letter sent acknowledging Henry's order;

ii) it is quite possible that Henry, although in law bound by the clause, was in fact unaware of it;

iii) there was no bargaining between the parties;

iv) the clause is too wide-ranging and all-embracing;

v) Ian ought to protect himself against liabilities of this nature by means of insurance.

On the alternative footing that Henry sells his furniture at a market stall, it is submitted that he still has a good claim against Ian because the latter's exclusion clause does not satisfy the requirement of reasonableness prescribed by the 1977 Act.

References

1) [1968] 1 WLR 1204
2) [1979] 1 WLR 401
3) (1877) 2 App Cas 666
4) (1877) 2 CPD 416
5) [1934] 2 KB 394
6) [1980] AC 627
7) [1983] 2 AC 802
8) [1915] 1 KB 73
9) [1978] 1 Lloyd's Rep 602

QUESTION 4

Suggested Solution

One must advise Kate whether she has any claim against Joanna for (a) breach of contract and (b) misrepresentation as a result of the statements made by Joanna prior to Kate's purchase of the shop and, if so, what remedies are available to Kate.

First, as to breach of contract, Joanna made three statements to Kate: in relation to the demand for health foods, the position vis-a-vis the local authority health inspectors and the profitability of the shop. Whether any or all of those statements can be regarded as terms of the contract of sale between Joanna and Kate depends upon the intention of the parties: *Heilbut Symonds & Co* v *Buckleton* (1), *Oscar Chess Ltd* v *Williams* (2) and *Dick Bentley Productions Ltd* v *Harold Smith (Motors) Ltd* (3). The sort of matters to which the court will have regard are the importance of the truth of the statement, the time which elapsed between the making of the statement and the conclusion of the contract; whether, if the contract was reduced to writing, the statement was included or omitted; and whether the maker of the statement was in a better position to know the truth.

Whilst it is difficult to be categorical on such matters, in the present case it is likely that the court would regard the statements made by Joanna as mere representations rather than terms of the contract: having regard to their form and character they do not look like statements which could have been reasonably understood to have contractual force. The contrary is not unarguable but on balance one must advise Kate that the statements were not terms of the contract.

Next, as to misrepresentation, each statement will be considered in turn.

As to Joanna's statement concerning the demand for health foods, at first sight this might appear not to be an actionable misrepresentation as it is a statement of opinion concerning the future behaviour of the market for health foods. However, it is not the case that a representation of opinion can never be an actionable misrepresentation of fact. Where the maker of a statement of opinion is in a better position to know the truth, he may be taken to have impliedly represented that he knew facts to justify his opinion: *Smith* v *Land* and *House Property Cor* (4) and *Brown* v *Raphael* (5). If such facts do not exist, he is guilty of a misrepresentation. Here, it is submitted, Joanna's first statement falls within this head of liability. As the owner of the shop she was in a position to know whether demand would increase or not, and the evidence known to her was that demand was falling, not rising. Accordingly, she has made a false statement of fact addressed to Kate. Providing this statement induced Kate to purchase the shop, in the sense that it was one reason for her doing so, *Edgington* v *Fitzmaurice* (6), she has a claim for misrepresentation.

As to the statement concerning there being no risk of trouble from health inspectors, it is submitted that this too is an actionable misrepresentation. Clearly, it is false, as the subsequent visit from the inspector has shown and it is a statement of mixed fact and law and accordingly actionable: *Cooper* v *Phibbs* (7). Misrepresentations as to the general law are not actionable, *Beattle* v *Lord Ebury* (8), but statements applying law to a particular set of facts is capable of being actionable, *Cooper*. Again, providing the requirement of inducement is satisfied, as on the facts it almost certainly will be, the second statement is also an actionable misrepresentation.

As to the profitability of the shop, it is submitted that this also is an actionable misrepresentation. Joanna's statement that it made 'up to £1,000 profit per week' is literally true, in that any profit below that figure is covered by the statement. However, this is a case in which the statement is a misleading half-truth, *Dimmock* v *Hallett* (9), since it conveys the impression that the shop regularly made a profit of around £1,000 when the true figure was far less. Nor does it matter that Kate did not inspect the accounts because a representee is under no duty to verify the accuracy of the representation made, *Redgrave* v *Hurd* (10).

In summary, on actionablity, one's advice to Kate is that all three statements constitute actionable misrepresentations.

Next we must consider the remedies available.

First, damages. The availability of the remedy of damages depends upon the nature of the misrepresentation committed, namely whether it was fraudulent, negligent or innocent. On the facts there is insufficient evidence to warrant a plea of fraud. As the speech of Lord Herschell in *Derry* v *Peek* (11) made clear, the essence of fraud is dishonesty and there is no proper evidence here of dishonesty on the part of Joanna.

On the other hand, there is probably a good claim for damages for negligent misrepresentation in that it is difficult to see how Joanna can establish that she had reasonable grounds for believing all three representations to be true. Certainly the first and the third appear to have been made negligently, which would enable Kate to recover damages under s2(1) of the Misrepresentation Act 1967. Section 2(1) imposes an absolute obligation on the representor not to make statements unless he has reasonable grounds for believing them to be true and the burden of proof is on the representor to establish these reasonable grounds.

If, as seems likely, Joanna cannot discharge this burden, Kate is entitled to damages under s2(1) calculated according to tortious out of pocket principles: *Andre et Cie* v *Michel Blanc* (12), *Chesneau* v *Interhome Ltd* (13) and *Sharneyford Supplies Ltd* v *Edge* (14). Kate is entitled to the difference between the contract price and the value of the business that she actually bought.

For completeness on negligence, one must add that it is unlikely that Kate could establish that a *Hedley Byrne* v *Heller* (15) type special relationship existed between her and Joanna so as to enable her to recover damages in tort for negligent misstatement, but in the light of her strong claim under s2(1) of the 1967 Act this does not much matter.

In addition to damages, Kate may well wish to rescind the contract. This involves restoring the parties to their respective pre-contractual positions and is effected by the representee giving notice thereof to the representor. The fact that the contract between Kate and Joanna has been executed is no longer a bar to rescission: s1(b) of the 1967 Act. Subject to the court's discretion under s2(2) referred to above, this seems an eminently suitable case for rescission providing Kate acts speedily to avoid the transaction. Although rescission involves institutio in integrum, the court is concerned to put the parties in broadly, rather than precisely, their pre-contractual positions and can, if necessary, order an account of profits and make allowances for deterioration: *Erlanger* v *New Sombrero Phosphate Co* (16).

If Kate is permitted to rescind, she will recover the purchase price paid to Joanna, and the shop will be reconveyed to the latter. Kate will also be entitled to an indemnity against obligations necessarily incurred by her as a result of having entered into the contract, which would include rates and other burdens imposed on an occupier of property: *Whittington* v *Seale-Hayne* (17), but this is a narrower form of financial relief than the remedy of damages.

In conclusion, Kate has a good claim for negligent misrepresentation for which she should recover damages under s2(1) of the 1967 Act and should also be able to rescind the contract.

References

1) [1913] AC 30
2) [1957] 1 WLR 370
3) [1965] 1 WLR 623
4) (1884) 28 Ch D 7
5) [1950] Ch 636
6) (1895) 29 Ch D 459
7) (1867) LR 2 HL 149
8) (1872) LR 7 Ch App 777
9) (1866) LR 2 Ch App 21
10) (1881) 20 Ch D 1
11) (1889) 14 App Cas 337
12) [1979] 2 Lloyd's Rep 427
13) (1983) The Times 9 June
14) [1985] 1 All ER 976
15) [1964] AC 465
16) (1878) 3 App Cas 1218
17) (1900) 82 LT 49

QUESTION 5

Suggested Solution

The extract from Lord Denning's judgment in *Magee* v *Penine Insurance* (1) echoes his Lordship's earlier statements of principles on the law of mistake in his judgment in *Solle* v *Butcher* (2). Properly to analyse this statement requires a discussion of, first, common mistake at law, and secondly, common mistake in equity.

In considering common mistake at law, his Lordship has always taken the radical view of the leading House of Lords case on the subject, *Bell* v *Lever Brothers Ltd* (3). His Lordship has consistently said that in Bell, the House of Lords decided that contracts are never void for common mistake. Whilst it is true that the decision on the facts was that the compensation agreements entered into between Bell and Snelling on the one hand, and Levers on the other, were not void for common mistake, it is respectfully submitted that his Lordship's approach is perhaps a little simplistic. Certainly *Bell* is a difficult case from which to extract a ratio decidendi, but it is suggested that in their speeches the majority were endeavouring to state the circumstances in which a contract would be void for common mistake. The fact that this may not have done so with the clarity one might have desired does no mean that there is no doctrine of common mistake at law.

His Lordship's view is also not one that has attracted widespread judicial or academic support. The normal approach to *Bell*'s case is to seek to derive from it a workable test as to when a contract will be void for common mistake, rather than to deny the possibility altogether. Thus Cheshire and Fifoot have argued that *Bell* decided that a contract will be void for common mistake whether its subject matter is, unknown to the parties, non-existent ('res extincta'). Whilst this may well be an example of a void contract, it may be doubted whether it is the only type of mistake that will suffice. The learned authors' reasoning is perhaps weakened by their reliance on *Couturier* v *Hastie* (4) which, as the Australian High Court convincingly demonstrated in *McRae* v *Commonwealth Disposals Commission* (5), turned on no more than the simple proposition that a seller who is unable to deliver a specific cargo is not entitled to recover the purchase price therefor from the buyer and was not really a case of mistake at all.

Alternatively Slade (6) has argued that a contract will only be void for common mistake where it is possible to imply a term into it that if certain assumed facts are incorrect, neither party is bound by the transaction. Whilst this view derives some support from the speech of Lord Atkin in *Bell*, ultimately it is not a satisfactory basis upon which to found the doctrine of mistake. The supposed term cannot be implied by any of the conventional tests (eg business efficacy, officious bystander, custom or usage or a necessary incident of the parties' legal relationship) and is artificial since it demands a good deal of judicial creativity to discover such a term in any contract.

Yet another approach, which gives a broader interpretation to *Bell* than that propounded by Lord Denning, is formulated by the editors of *Chitty on Contracts* (7). They suggest that mistake is all about the allocation of risk. Ordinarily, one or other party will have taken the risk that certain facts which are assumed to be true are not true, and in such a case there is no room for the operation of the doctrine of mistake. Where, however, on the true construction of the contract neither party has taken that risk so, it is said, the contract is void for mistake.

This view commended itself to Sir John Pennycuick in *Amalgamated Investment & Property Co Ltd* v *John Walker & Sons Ltd* (8) and is to some extent at least consistent with the tenor of the speeches of the majority in *Bell*. It can also be reconciled with some of the older pre-*Bell* mistake cases such as *Hitchcock* v *Giddings* (9) (res extincta), *Cooper* v *Phibbs* (10) (mistake as to title) and *Gompertz* v *Bartlett* (11) (mistake as to quality). Also, *McRae* can be regarded as a case in which the sellers, having warranted the existence of the vessel, took the risk that it did not exist and were therefore liable in damages to the buyers.

Thus to conclude on the common law, one can say that, with respect to Lord Denning, his statement probably does not accurately reflect the law of England.

Turning next to equity, the first case unequivocally to establish that a contract which is not void at law for common mistake may nevertheless be voidable in equity was *Solle* v *Butcher*, where Denning LJ (as he then was) said that a contract was liable to be set aside if the parties were under a common misapprehension either as to facts or as to their relative and respective rights, providing the misapprehension was fundamental and the party seeking to set aside the transaction was not at fault. Whilst the authorities from which the court sought to derive this principle perhaps did not justify their radical innovation, since *Solle* this new equitable jurisdiction has become firmly established. In particular it has been considered and applied in these later cases, *Grist* v *Bailey* (12), *Magee* v *Penine Insurance* and *Lawrence* v *Lexcourt Holdings Ltd* (13). The new jurisdiction holds that a contract may be voidable for common mistake in equity even though it is valid at law and, moreover, that the court can impose terms upon which equitable relief is granted.

Although Lord Denning has suggested that equity has supplanted the common law entirely, it is submitted that unless and until *Bell* is reconsidered by the House of Lords, that case remains authority for the proposition that contracts may be void for common mistake, albeit in limited and uncertain circumstances. The happiest reconciliation of *Bell* on the one hand and *Solle* and the subsequent equity cases on the other may be that suggested by Goff J (as he then was) in *Grist* v *Bailey*. First, his Lordship asked himself whether the contract was void at law and, holding that *Bell* confined mistake at law within very narrow limits, decided it was not. Secondly, his Lordship then asked whether the contract was nevertheless voidable in equity, where the test is less rigorous. On the facts his Lordship concluded that the parties' mistake (as to the security of terms enjoyed by the occupant of a house being offered for sale) was sufficiently fundamental to justify the grant of relief in equity.

Thus, to conclude, in terms of strict legal theory, it is respectfully suggested that Lord Denning's statement in *Magee* is incorrect and that contracts may be void for common mistake, not merely voidable. In practical terms, however, the problems posed by an analysis of *Bell* and the now flourishing equitable doctrine of mistake stemming from *Solle* means that it is to equity rather than the common law that litigants will look in seeking relief from a common mistake.

References

1) [1969] 2 QB 507
2) [1950] 1 KB 671
3) [1932] AC 161
4) (1856) 9 Ex 102
5) (1951) 84 CLR 377
6) (1954) 70 LQR 388
7) 25th edition para 318
8) [1977] 1 WLR 164
9) (1817) Dan 1
10) (1867) LR 2 HL 149
11) (1853) 2 E & B 849

References (continued)

12) [1967] Ch 532
13) [1978] 1 WLR 1128

QUESTION 6

Suggested Solution

Linda has entered into three transactions, which will be discussed in turn:

a) the modelling lessons;

b) the purchase of the sewing machine;

c) the purchase of the shares.

a) *Modelling lessons*

Linda is aged 17 and is therefore an infant or minor: s1 of the Family Law Reform Act 1969. The effect of her minority is that, with certain limited exceptions, she is incapable of entering into binding contracts. One of those exceptions, based on the common law, is that a minor is capable of entering into a binding contract of service, providing it is of a beneficial nature. The modelling lessons may well fall into this category.

Beneficial contracts of service are contracts which are generally of an educational or instructive nature, as this allows a minor to earn his living by becoming proficient at some trade or calling eg singing lessons in *Mackinlay* v *Bathurst* (1) or a contract between an infant boxer and the British Boxing Board of Control in *Doyle* v *White City Stadium Ltd* (2). Providing the contract is, taken overall, beneficial, the minor will be bound, *Clements* v *London and North Western Railway* (3) and *De Francesco* v *Barnum* (4). Moreover the minor is liable even though the contract is executory or partially executed only, *Roberts* v *Gray* (5).

The question to be determined here is whether the modelling lessons can be regarded as a beneficial contract of service for a minor who is a student of fashion design. If Linda wished to become a model, then as long as the contract was beneficial overall, she would be bound. The difficulty arises from the fact that the lessons have, at best, only a peripheral bearing on her intended career. She may have thought that the lessons would assist her, but that is not the test: rather she must ask whether the contract will in some way assist Linda to find her way in life.

Although the point is not free from difficulty it is submitted that there is just a sufficient connection between Linda's course of study and the modelling lessons to warrant the conclusion that it was a contract of service capable of binding Linda and, in the absence of any evidence that its terms were not beneficial – £200 does not seem excessive – she is therefore bound by it and must pay the price of the lessons. One's conclusion is fortified by the trend of recent decisions concerning minors to broaden rather than narrow the scope of a minor's liability (eg *Chaplin* v *Leslie Frewin (Publishers) Ltd* (6)), perhaps reflecting the view that much of the law relating to minors is anomalous and needs to be reformed. One's advice to Linda is, therefore, that she will probably be held liable to pay the price of the lessons.

b) *The sewing machine*
In considering the sewing machine, one must discuss two statutory provisions, s3 of the Sale of Goods Act 1979 and s1 of the Infants Relief Act 1874, to determine Linda's liability, if any, under this contract.

Section 3(2) of the 1979 Act provides that where necessaries are sold and delivered to a minor he must pay a reasonable price for them, and sub-section (3) defines necessaries as meaning goods suitable to the condition in life of the minor and to his actual requirements at the time of sale and delivery. Since the contract is executed, the familiar problem of whether a minor is liable on an executory contract for necessary goods does not arise, and the sole issue for discussion is whether the sewing machine is a necessary.

Reported cases are of little assistance because each case turns on its particular facts and, further, most reported decisions concerning necessary goods are nineteenth century cases which are of no or little relevance today. Looking at the matter as one of principle, it is submitted that the purchase of a de luxe sewing machine for £300 is not a necessary as defined by s3(3) of the 1979 Act for a seventeen year old first year fashion student; it may be useful or even desirable, but it is not, strictly speaking, a necessary.

As the machine is not a necessary, the contract is therefore governed by s1 of the 1874 Act which provides that all contracts with minors for goods supplied or to be supplied, other than necessaries, are 'absolutely void'. At first blush this expression would seem to indicate that the contract is devoid of any legal effect that Linda is not obliged to pay the price and that she is bound to return the machine. However, the few cases that there are on s1 have not always given the words 'absolutely void' their ordinary meaning. Thus in *Valentini* v *Canali* (7) and *Pearce* v *Brain* (8) it was said that money paid under an 'absolutely void' contract by the minor was only recoverable if there had been a total failure of consideration or, at least, the minor had derived no benefit thereunder. Further, in *Stocks* v *Wilson* (9) Lush J expressed the view that despite the language of s1, property in non-necessary goods will pass to the minor on delivery. Although Lush J's view was an obiter dictum, it has generally been accepted as being correct; in terms of policy it has the merit of protecting an innocent third party purchaser from the minor. The cumulative effect of *Valentini, Pearce* and *Stocks* in the present case is that property in the machine has passed to Linda and since there has been no fortune of consideration, or at any rate Linda has enjoyed a benefit under the contract viz. rights of ownership in and the use of the machine, she is not entitled to recover the purchase price she paid for it. Although this conclusion may seem to rest a little oddly with the wording of s1 the present state of the authorities permits no other answer.

c) *The shares*

A contract for the acquisition of shares in a company by a minor is voidable and binds the minor unless and until it is repudiated either during minority or within a reasonable time of attaining his or her majority, *North Western Railway Co* v *McMichael* (10). Thus as Linda is still a minor, it is open to her to repudiate the contract between her and Melvyn. What is less certain is the legal effect of such repudiation.

As between Linda and the company, any future obligations owed by her as shareholder (eg in respect of calls on the shares) will be discharged, but in *Steinberg* v *Scala* (11) the view was expressed that repudiation is not retrospective and that the minor remains liable for accrued obligations. Whilst *McMichael's* case suggests otherwise, the view in *Steinberg* would probably be preferred by the court.

As between Linda and Melvyn, *Steinberg's* case suggests that she will not be entitled to recover the money paid to him and that the sole effect of repudiation is to discharge the minor from future obligations. This is consistent with cases dealing with other types of voidable contracts eg *Corpe* v *Overton* (12) (partnership) and *Holmes* v *Blogg* (13) (a lease). Linda therefore cannot recover the money paid by her to Melvyn.

References

1) (1919) 36 TLR 31
2) [1935] 1 KB 110

References (continued)

3) [1894] 2 QB 482
4) (1890) 45 Ch D 430
5) [1913] 1 KB 520
6) [1966] Ch 71
7) (1889) 24 QBD 166
8) [1929] 2 KB 310
9) [1913] 2 KB 235
10) (1850) 5 Ex 114
11) [1923] 2 Ch 452
12) (1833) 10 Bing 252
13) (1818) 8 Taunt 35

QUESTION 7

Suggested Solution

The statement refers to the doctrine of privity of contract and in considering it the following will be discussed:

a) the general rule;

b) exceptions to it; and

c) how the law may be developed in future cases.

The general rule

The rule that a person cannot acquire enforceable rights under a contract to which he is not a party, even though it may have been made for his benefit, is considered to have been conclusively established in 1861 in the case of *Tweddle* v *Atkinson* (1) where the fathers of a bride and groom agreed with each other to pay certain sums to the groom, adding that the groom should have the power to recover those sums by action if either failed to pay. The bride's father defaulted and the groom sued, but his action failed on the grounds (inter alia) that he was not a party to the contract.

The rule in *Tweddle* v *Atkinson* has been affirmed by the House of Lords on three separate occasions this century, namely *Dunlop Pneumatic Tyre Co Ltd* v *Selfridge & Co Ltd* (2), *Scruttons Ltd* v *Midland Silicones Ltd* (3) and *Beswick* v *Beswick* (4). In the latter case their Lordships disagreed with the conclusion of the Court of Appeal that s56(1) of the Law of Property Act 1925 had abolished the doctrine of privity and expressed the view that the sub-section created only a limited exception in the law of real property. Although in *Woodar Investment Development Co Ltd* v *Wimpey Construction UK Ltd* (5) certain remarks were made by their Lordships about the desirability of overruling *Tweddle* v *Atkinson,* unless and until this is done by the House, or the legislature chooses to amend the law by statute, *Tweddle* is binding authority on all inferior courts that a stranger cannot sue on a contract to which he is not a party.

The practical consequences of the rule can often be that a considerable injustice is suffered. Not only can the third party not sue, the promisee also cannot sue to recover damages on behalf of the third party unless a relationship of trust or agency exists. In

Jackson v *Horizon Holidays Ltd* (6) Lord Denning held that *Lloyds* v *Harper* (7) established the principle that a promisee who made a contract for the benefit of a third party can recover damages on the latter's behalf. This judgment was strongly disapproved by all five members of the House in *Woodar* v *Wimpey* and although *Jackson* was technically not overruled, it seems inconceivable that it would be followed in future cases. Henceforth *Lloyds* v *Harper* is to be regarded as dealing with relationships of trust or agency only and, in consequence, the third party's loss will be uncompensated. In *Forster* v *Silvermere Golf and Equestrian Centre Ltd* (8) Dillon J said this result was a blot on the law and most unjust; it remains, nevertheless, the law.

A means of avoiding this injustice and preventing the third party's loss not being remedied was utilised in *Beswick* v *Beswick* where the plaintiff, the promisee's widow, was able as his administratrix to obtain specific performance against the defendant, the promisor, in her own favour as third party beneficiary, thereby preventing the defendant from breaking his contract with impunity. However, specific performance is a discretionary remedy and not automatically granted, and although the court might be strongly minded to order it so as to prevent injustice occurring, it will not always be possible eg as in *Woodsar* v *Wimpey* where the contract had been terminated and was not capable of being specifically enforced.

Exceptions

Because of the injustice that may flow from a strict application of the rule in *Tweddle* v *Atkinson,* there are many exceptions to it, statutory, equitable and at common law. Some are true exceptions and others are devices adopted by the courts to circumvent the rule.

Of the statutory exceptions, reference has already been made to s56(1) of the 1925 Act. Whilst their Lordships in *Beswick* did not speak with one voice as to the true construction of that sub-section, the predominant view was that it only applied in the law of real property where there is a purported grant to or covenant with a named person who is not a party to the instrument.

Other important statutory exceptions are contained in the law of insurance, in particular the Married Women's Property Act 1882 s11, the Road Traffic Act 1972 s148(4), the Marine Insurance Act 1906 s14(2) and the Fires Prevention (Metropolis) Act 1774) s83. These, in one field of insurance or another, allow an action to be maintained on an insurance policy by a person who is not a party to it.

The most important equitable exception is that of a trust: where A makes a promise to B for the benefit of C, C can enforce the promise if B has been instituted trustee of the promise for C: *Tomlinson* v *Gee* (9) and *Les Affreteur Reunis* v *Leopold Walford (London) Ltd* (10). Whilst the concept of a trust of a contractual right is straightforward and comprehensible, determining in any particular case whether one has been created can be a question of considerable difficulty and leave much room for judicial ingenuity.

For a trust to be instituted the 'three certainties' must be present ie of intention, subject matter and objects. In contract, it is the former that gives rise to the most difficulty, since it is rare for the promisor and promisee to make their intention clear in the terms of their agreement. Accordingly the question is often one of inference: whether one can impute to them an irrevocable intention to benefit the third party. Irrevocability is vital, since once a trust is created it is enforceable by the beneficiary and cannot be dissolved or determined by the settlor or the trustee or both.

The difficulty of deducing the parties' intentions has led to different conclusions being reached in cases involving broadly similar facts eg *Re Flavell* (11) and *Re Schebsman* (12). Taking a broad view of the trust cases it is probably fair to say that at one time the trust of a contractual right was a device commonly used to circumvent the doctrine of privity, but that often it was no more than device, and it involved attributing to the parties an intention they almost certainly never possessed. Now, by contrast, it seems no longer to be in favour.

Other exceptions, apparent or real, are the doctrine of agency, including the rules relating to undisclosed principals; collateral contracts, which may be used to 'construct' a contract (eg *Shanklin Pier Ltd* v *Detel Products Ltd* (13)); and by established commercial practices which the courts are reluctant to upset, particularly the proposition that the bank is liable to pay on presentation by the seller of the proper shipping documents, although it is doubtful whether in terms of strict legal analysis a contract exists between them (eg *Hamzeh Malas & Sons* v *British Imex Industries Ltd* (14)).

Reform

As long ago as 1937, the Law Revision Committee in its 6th Interim Report recommended the abolition of the rule in *Tweddle* v *Atkinson* and that third parties should be entitled to enforce contracts made for their benefit, providing certain conditions were satisfied. Since then, two decisions of the House of Lords, *Scruttons* and *Beswick* have spurned this opportunity. However, in the latest privity case to reach their Lordships' House, *Woodar* v *Wimpey*, there was a significant shift in judicial thinking. Although the point did not fall squarely for consideration, Lords Salmon, Keith and Scarman all said, obiter, that the time had come to reconsider and probably reverse the rule in *Tweddle* v *Atkinson*, and that if the legislature did not soon take this step then their Lordships' House should consider doing so. It seems, therefore, that the days of that rule may now be numbered.

Conclusion

It is submitted that the statement is broadly correct, though it is a general rule subject to exceptions rather than being an absolute one. Further, it is a rule which, it appears, may now be retaining only a precarious foothold in English law.

References

1) (1861) 1 B & S 393
2) [1915] AC 847
3) [1962] AC 446
4) [1968] AC 58
5) [1980] 1 WLR 277
6) [1975] 1 WLR 1468
7) (1880) 16 Ch D 270
8) (1981) 125 SJ 397
9) (1756) Amb 330
10) [1919] AC 801
11) (1883) 25 Ch D 89
12) [1944] Ch 83
13) [1951] 2 KB 854
14) [1958] 2 QB 127

QUESTION 8

Suggested Solution

The doctrine referred to in the question is known as frustration, which is the term used to describe a situation where, owing to a change of circumstances occurring after the conclusion of the contract, both parties are discharged from their outstanding obligations by operation of law; in such a case the contract is said to be frustrated.

The question requires a discussion of the circumstances in which the doctrine of frustration will be held to apply, and in particular whether actual impossibility of performance is required or whether something less might suffice.

The case which first introduced the doctrine of frustration in 1963, *Taylor* v *Caldwell* (1), was a case of physical impossibility. Prior to that date English law had always regarded contractual obligations as being absolute and as continuing to bind the parties irrespective of the effect of extraneous events, as in *Paradine* v *Jane* (2). In *Taylor* it was held that a licence to use a music hall was frustrated when the building was destroyed by a fire for which neither party was responsible. The Court of Queen's Bench said that it was an implied condition of the contract that the building should continue to exist and, on its destruction, both parties were discharged from further performance.

The law has moved on from *Taylor* in two significant respects. First, the theory that frustration depends upon an implied term to that effect forming a part of the contract can no longer be regarded as good law, and secondly, it is possible for a contract still to be physically possible of performance but frustrated in law because the commercial purpose of adventure is no longer possible of performance. These two developments in the law will be discussed in turn.

As to the theory that frustration depended upon there being an implied term in the contract, it has been seen that the doctrine owes its very existence to the court in *Taylor* finding such a term and, further, this view commanded a good deal of support for a considerable number of years: *FA Tamplin SS Co Ltd* v *Anglo-Mexican Petroleum Products Co Ltd* (3) and *Bank Line Ltd* v *Arthur*

Capel & Co (4) are charterparty cases in which the House of Lords applied the implied term approach.

Judicially, however, the implied term theory was not found to be satisfactory, in that there was no rational legal basis for implying or not implying the necessary terms. Its implication could not be justified by any subjective test, since if the parties had foreseen the frustrating event they would almost certainly have made provision for it. Alternatively, to imply it objectively involves much artificiality as it involves attributing to the parties an intention which they never had in relation to an event which, on hypothesis, they did not foresee.

It was for this reason that the courts subsequently discarded the implied term approach in favour of, as it is now known, the radical change in the obligation test, which derives from the decision of the House of Lords and in particular the speech of Viscount Radcliffe, in *Davis Contractors Ltd* v *Fareham UDC* (5). His Lordship stated that frustration occurs whenever the law recognises that, without default in either party, a contractual obligation has become incapable of being performed because the circumstances in which performance is called for would render it a thing radically different from that which was undertaken by the contract: 'Non haec in foedera veni. It was not this that I promised to do' (6).

This statement of principle has recently been approved in two further decisions of their Lordships' House, *National Carriers Ltd* v *Panalpina Northern) Ltd* (7) and *The Nema* (8), and can accordingly now be regarded as settled law. Other judicial analyses as to the judicial basis of the doctrine eg the just and reasonable solution (per Denning LJ in *British Movietonews Ltd* v *London and District Cinemas Ltd* (9)) and the disappearance of the foundation of the contract theories (per Goddard J in *Tatem Ltd* v *Gamboa* (10)) can now be discarded.

Davis v *Fareham* is also of interest in that it is a good illustration of the principle that merely because a contract has become more onerous or expensive for one side to perform does not justify a finding of frustration: delay caused by bad weather and shortages of skilled labour which rendered the contract unprofitable for the appellants did not discharge the contract. Thus it is correct to say that where the unforeseen events simply make performance more burdensome, frustration does not apply.

Nevertheless, turning to the second point above mentioned, it may be doubted whether actual impossibility is a necessary requirement for the application of the doctrine. Although Viscount Radcliffe's speech in *Davis* v *Fareham* does refer to a contract obligation being 'incapable of performance' and, as such, would appear to support a test of physical impossibilities only, it is submitted that read as a whole his Lordship's speech does not support such a proposition. In particular, his Lordship contemplated that the contract might still be capable (ie not impossible) of performance but frustrated because the changed circumstances mean that the obligation, if performed, would be a different thing from that contracted for. Further, it is submitted that this is borne out in any number of reported frustration cases.

One might point to cases such as *Jackson* v *Union Marine Insurance Co Ltd* (11), where a ship under charter ran aground and required repairs which took some eight months, and *Krell* v *Henry* (12), where a contract to hire rooms to view the coronation procession of King Edward VII was held to be frustrated when the event was cancelled, were cases in which physical performance are still possible, but the supervening events had rendered the nature of the contractual obligation fundamentally different. Moreover the recent recognition by the House of Lords in the *National Carriers* case that leases may, albeit only in exceptional circumstances, be frustrated also lends support to this view. Once a lease is executed, the legal estate vests in the tenant irrespective of what might happen thereafter, so in that sense, there is no impossibility, yet the lease is, as the House of Lords held, capable of being frustrated.

However, one must add the caveat that although strict impossibility is not always required, the court will almost certainly require something falling not far short of it before allowing the doctrine of frustration to be invoked. The courts are reluctant to allow parties to escape their contractual obligations except in the very clearest of cases. The Suez cases concerning charterparties and contracts for the sale of goods which became more expensive of performance as a result of the closure of the Suez Canal, *The Eugenia* (13) and *Tsakiroglou & Co Ltd* v *Noblee Thorl* (14) being good examples of this.

In conclusion, therefore, one would say certainly that where the unforeseen events merely render performance more burdensome, the contract is not frustrated, but the strict physical impossibility is not always necessary.

References

1) (1863) 3 B & S 826
2) (1646) Aleyn 26
3) [1916] 2 AC 397

References (continued)

4) [1919] AC 435
5) [1956] AC 696
6) ibid at p729
7) [1981] AC 675
8) [1982] AC 724
9) [1951] 1 KB 190, revsd [1952] AC 166
10) [1939] 1 KB 132
11) (1874) LR 10 CP 125
12) [1903] 2 KB 740
13) [1964] 2 QB 226
14) [1962] AC 93

QUESTION 9

Suggested Solution

Olive is claiming to recover damages from Paul in respect of four heads of loss, namely:

a) air fares;

b) hotel bills;

c) cost of a nanny;

d) emotional distress.

The validity of each of these claims will be discussed in turn.

a) *Air fares*

Plainly this head of loss was caused by Paul's breach of contract. That, however, is not sufficient to render the expense recoverable from Paul. In addition, Olive must show that the loss falls within the rule in *Hadley* v *Baxendale* (1) as explained in later cases and is not too remote; also, questions of mitigation may arise.

In considering principles of remoteness, the important question to ask is whether Paul knew, at the time he entered into the contract with Olive, that she had a house and family in London but had been appointed to a position in Manchester and required the new house for that purpose. The state of Paul's knowledge is important because for loss to be recoverable as damages for breach of contract it must have been in the reasonable contemplation of the parties at the time they entered into the contract as having been the probable result of its breach, *Hadley* v *Baxendale*.

As explained by the Court of Appeal in *Victoria Laundry Ltd* v *Newman Industries Ltd* (2), the parties' knowledge is all important and is of two types, imputed and actual. Everybody is taken to possess the former and to know the usual course of things (the first limb of the rule in *Hadley* v *Baxendale*), the latter is knowledge of special circumstances which makes additional loss likely. This part of the Court's judgment was not disapproved in *The Heron II* (3) and is accordingly still good law. Moreover, it is sufficient that, given the knowledge of the parties, the head of loss is a 'serious possibility', a phrase used by a number of their Lordships in *The Heron II* and subsequently adopted as the test for remoteness of damage in contract by Orr and Scarman LJJ in *Parsons (Livestock Ltd)* v *Uttley Ingham & Co Ltd* (4).

It is submitted that the expense of air fares incurred by Olive cannot be regarded as being in the ordinary course of things, because it is quite possible that a person purchasing a property in Manchester already lives nearby and not in London (cf the possibility in *Hadley* v *Baxendale* that the plaintiffs might have had another mill shaft).

However, if Paul did know of Olive's personal circumstances then he must be advised he did have actual knowledge of special circumstances that made additional loss likely: there must have been a serious possibility that Olive would feel it necessary to commute from London to Manchester and back. However, it cannot sensibly be argued that she was acting unreasonably and failing in her duty to mitigate by flying rather than using some other form of transport, or in doing so every weekend. The duty to mitigate requires a plaintiff to act reasonably, *British Westinghouse Electric Co Ltd* v *Underground Electric Rys* (5), and in all the circumstances there is little prospect of persuading the court that Olive acted unreasonably.

b) *Hotel bills*

Where, due to a builder's breach of contract, a purchaser of a house is unable to occupy the property by the contractual completion date, it must be a serious possibility that in the ordinary course of things (the first limb of the rule in *Hadley* v *Baxendale*) the purchaser will incur expense in obtaining alternative accommodation for the interim. Further, so long as the type of loss is one that might have been contemplated by the parties, it is irrelevant that the extent of it could not: *Wroth* v *Tyler* (6). Thus in principle it is clear that the cost of alternative accommodation is a head of loss recoverable by Olive from Paul. The position is a fortiori if Paul in fact knew that Olive's former home was in London.

On the other hand there is a substantial argument that can be raised on Paul's behalf that in staying at a five-star hotel Olive has not acted reasonably in mitigating her loss: *British Westinghouse*. Unless Olive can demonstrate that there was no other suitable accommodation available, it is submitted that the court would conclude that Olive acted with unreasonable extravagance in staying at a five-star hotel and will award her a lesser sum than that in fact expended by her, assessed by reference to a more reasonable and less luxurious style of accommodation.

c) *Nanny*

Olive may run into difficulties on the question of causation in respect of sums paid by her to a nanny. As she was a working woman with children she would, presumably, have engaged a nanny to care for them during the day whether she was based in London or Manchester. This therefore was an item of expenditure which she would have incurred in any event and is therefore not recoverable from Paul.

She may, however, have a good claim in respect of monies paid to the nanny on those evenings when she was in Manchester, or alternatively in transit to or from London, since this additional expenditure would plainly be caused by Paul's breach of contract. The considerations as to remoteness which arise are the same as those discussed in connection with the air fares above. If Paul had knowledge of Olive's personal circumstances at the time the contract was concluded, then the loss would fall within the second limb of the rule in *Hadley* v *Baxendale* and be recoverable from him. If he was unaware of the relevant facts, again it is submitted that the court would regard the loss as being too remote.

d) *Distress*

Until relatively recently the decision of the House of Lords in *Addis* v *Gramaphone Co* (7) was considered to lay down the rule that distress or disappointment was not a head of loss for which damages could be awarded in contract. However, in a succession of recent cases the application of the *Addis* principle has been considerably narrowed and it is now widely regarded as dealing only with claims for damages for distress consequent upon an employee being wrongfully dismissed and not laying down a general rule which applies throughout the law of contract.

The cases which have established that damages for distress may be awarded, providing the normal test as to remoteness is satisfied are, in chronological order: *Jarvis* v *Swans Tours* (8); *Jackson* v *Horizon Holidays* (9); *Heywood* v *Wellers* (10); *Cox* v *Philips Industries* (11) and *Perry* v *Sidney Phillips & Son* (12). Taken together, they establish that the courts have a general jurisdiction to award damages for distress caused by a breach of contract if it is not too remote.

Here the distress suffered by Olive is due to her being separated from her family and not due to the delay itself. Again issues of remoteness arise. Depending upon whether or not Paul was aware that Olive had a family living in London, the distress might be regarded as being either a serious possibility, which could have been contemplated, or conversely, too remote. Though if Olive were to establish that Paul knew she had a family in London, he should not be too concerned by her claim to recover a 'substantial sum'. Although damages are now awarded for distress, the sums awarded are not extravagant and tend to be in hundreds rather than thousands.

References

1) (1854) 9 Ex 341
2) [1949] 2 KB 528
3) [1969] 1 AC 350
4) [1978] QB 791
5) [1912] AC 673
6) [1974] Ch 30
7) [1909] AC 488
8) [1973] 1 QB 233
9) [1975] 1 WLR 1468
10) [1976] QB 446
11) [1976] 1 WLR 638
12) [1982] 1 WLR 1297

UNIVERSITY OF LONDON
INTERMEDIATE EXAMINATION IN LAWS 1986
for External Students

ELEMENTS OF THE LAW OF CONTRACT

Friday, 20th June: 10.00 am to 1.00 pm

Answer *FIVE* of the following NINE questions.

1 On Wednesday, 1st May an announcement appears in the morning newspapers to the effect that shares in Natoil, an oil exploration company, may be subscribed for at one pound each.

That day Slick sees the announcement and fills in the application form in the newspaper requesting 1,000 shares. He posts the application on the same day together with a cheque for £1,000. His application is received by the company the following day and the Secretary promptly sends the share certificates to Slick by that morning's post. However, Slick changes his mind and on the same afternoon (ie Thursday) he posts a letter to that effect to the company.

During the day a rich oil source is discovered by the Company in the North Sea and the Secretary telephones Slick informing him that they do not wish to accept his application and would like him to return the certificates when they arrive.

By now Slick has heard of the oil discovery and wishes to buy the shares after all.

Advise Slick.

2 a) E was attending a business conference in a town 200 miles from his home in London. As the conference finished late and there were no more trains to London that evening E asked a colleague F, who was driving to London, if F could give him (E) a lift. F agreed and when E got out of the car in London he promised to pay F £20 for the petrol. E has failed to pay the £20. Advise F.

b) G is the tenant of a flat owned by H. The rent is £400 a month payable on the lst of the month. On June 3 G told H that he could not afford to pay so much this month. H replied 'Give me £250 and we'll say no more about it.' G gave H £250. G has now received a letter from H demanding immediate payment of the balance of the rent for June. Advise G.

3 J made a contract with K, a builder, for K to build an extension to J's house for a price of £8,000 to be paid on completion. The contract stated: 'It is a condition of this contract that all work will be performed with proper skill and care and that the house will remain habitable throughout the period of the works.'

The work was estimated to take six weeks to complete. Two weeks after work started J learned that other local builders would have done the same job for £6,000. A week after that L, a labourer employed by K, carelessly fractured a water pipe: the house was flooded and J and his family were forced to leave it for three days. J hereupon informed K that he regarded the contract as cancelled, but K wishes to complete the job. Advise K.

4 a) 'Mistake as to the attributes of the other contracting party does not make the contract void.'

Explain and comment.

b) M walks into N's art gallery and expresses interest in a painting for sale at £10,000. M says she would like to have the painting and tells N that she is Lady Cynthia Warburton and that she represents the well-known firm of Warburton & Co Ltd. M produces a cheque book with Warburton & Co Ltd's name printed on it (which she had stolen earlier that day) and N allows her to take the painting away in return for a cheque signed by her on behalf of Warburton & Co Ltd.

The cheque has now been dishonoured and M has disappeared, after selling the painting to O for £9,500.

Advise N.

5 a) 'The rule of the common law is that where a party sustains a loss by breach of contract, he is, so far as money can do it, to be placed in the same position as if the contract had been performed.' (*Robinson* v *Harman* (1848)).

Discuss.

b) Bill, a business tycoon, contacted a hire firm who provide chauffeured executive cars and booked a car for 6 am the following day to take him to Heathrow Airport from where he was booked to travel to New York with the intention of signing a multi-million dollar contract. The driver lost his way and arrived so late that Bill missed the flight and the opportunity of obtaining the contract.

Advise Bill.

6 Percy replied to Victor's advertisement for the sale of his small printing business. Victor has been ill for the last year and the business has been run by a manager. When Percy came to see him, Victor said that the business was 'in excellent order'. When Percy asked to see the books Victor said 'You can see them if you wish but I assure you that profits have regularly topped £500 per week. Demand is exceptionally high and likely to remain so for the foreseeable future.' The figure quoted was in fact correct but recent figures indicated a likely downturn in business.

Victor's accountant had recently written to the firm warning of the need to invest heavily in new technology if the business was to survive.

Percy went ahead and bought the business which is now about to collapse unless there is substantial investment.

Advise Percy.

7 a) 'Even if there is a radical change of circumstances a contract is not necessarily frustrated.'

Comment.

b) Fred arranged with Len, a retired law lecturer, to give Fred's son, Simon, a course of two one hour lessons a week for ten weeks to prepare him for his Law of Contract examination. It was agreed that Fred would pay Len £50 at the beginning of the course and a further £150 at the end.

After five lessons Simon had a nervous breakdown and was obviously not going to be able to take the examination. Fred therefore cancelled the rest of the course. Len had spent a considerable amount of time preparing the classes and had bought the latest edition of the set text books.

Advise Len.

8 Tom, a businessman, regularly stayed at the Hotel Splendide whenever he visited London on business. He stayed there last week. As usual there was a notice on the back of his room door stating that 'Neither the Hotel Splendide nor any of its management or other employees will be responsible for any personal injury, loss or other damage to guests or their property howsoever caused.'

The day after he arrived Tom's car was stolen from the hotel car park after a porter who was parking the car had left the key in the ignition and the door unlocked. On hearing of this and going to investigate, Tom slipped on the highly polished corridor outside his room and suffered considerable injury to his back, and his valuable wristwatch struck the floor and was destroyed.

Advise Tom.

9 Referring to infants' contracts it has been said that 'The law on this topic is based on two principles. The first, and more important, is that the law must protect the infant against his own inexperience, ... the second principle is that the law should not cause unnecessary hardship to adults who deal fairly with infants.' (Treitel).

Explain how the law gives effect to these principles and consider how, if necessary, the law might usefully be reformed.

QUESTION 1

Suggested Solution

In advising Slick it is necessary to consider whether or not there has been a concluded contract for the sale of the shares between himself and the company.

It is clear that the announcement in the newspaper constitutes an invitation to treat and not offer, *Partridge* v *Crittenden* (1). Slick's application constitutes the offer to purchase the shares. It is equally clear that, having completed the prescribed form and paid the required sum, Slick's actions amount to a firm offer.

The next point to consider is whether Slick's offer has been accepted. The sending of the share certificates to Slick is an act of acceptance. What has to be considered is whether and when this acceptance has been communicated to Slick, in the light of the rule relating to acceptances through the post. The rule, established in *Adams* v *Lindsell* (2), is that, where there has been communication through the post, the acceptance is complete as soon as it has been posted. This rule has been consistently affirmed, see for example *Household Fire Insurance Co Ltd* v *Grant* (3), *Henthorn* v *Fraser* (4), *Brinkibon Ltd* v *Stahag Stahl* (5). There is, at this stage, no suggestion that the normal postal rule has been displaced, as where the offerer prescribes that he should receive actual notice of the acceptance as in *Holwell Securities Ltd* v *Hughes* (6). Accordingly the application of the postal rule would mean that the contract is concluded when the secretary posts the share certificates to Slick on the morning of Thursday, 2nd May.

Slick has, however, purported to revoke his offer, Whilst an offer may be revoked at any time before acceptance, there must be actual communication of the revocation to the offeree before it has been accepted. The application of the ratio in *Byrne* v *Van Tienhoven* (7) requires the answer here that, the revocation of the offer having been communicated after acceptance, this purported revocation must be deemed to be ineffective.

It appears further that the Company has attempted to withdraw its acceptance after it has been posted, but before it has come to the notice of Slick. There is no clear authority in English law on whether an offeree can withdraw his acceptance, after it has been posted, by a swifter method of communication. The strict application of the postal rule would suggest that withdrawal is not allowed. There are decisions to this effect in New Zealand in *Wenkheim* v *Arndt* (8) and South Africa in *A-Z Bazaars (Pty) Ltd* v *Minister of Agriculture* (9). And it does seem contrary to principle to hold the offeror bound as soon as the acceptance has been posted and yet to permit the offeree to withdraw. The contrary view is forcibly argued by Professor Hudson. He holds that the postal rule is merely one of convenience and ought not to be inflexibly applied. He says that if the offeror takes 'the risks of delay and accident in the post, it would not seem to strain matters to say that he also assumes the risk of a letter being overtaken by a speedier means of communication.'

Although there is a merit in Professor Hudson's argument it might apply where the offeror has chosen the post as a means of communication and not to the present situation where it is arguably the Company which has elected to receive offers through the post and should therefore be bound by the postal rule in all its rigour.

The strict application of *Byrne* v *Van Tienhoven* and the postal rule would, therefore lead to the conclusion that there is a binding contract for the sale of the shares which would afford Slick an action for specific performance, or alternatively, a claim in damages. However, in *Holwell Securities Ltd* v *Hughes* Lawton LJ observed that the postal rule does not apply if its application would produce manifest inconvenience and absurdity. It may well be that the court would find that such inconvenience and absurdity resulted from its application where, as in the present instance, both parties clearly showed their intention of withdrawing from the contract. Moreover the traditional analysis of offer and acceptance has been criticised by Lord Denning MR in *Gibson* v *Manchester City Council* (10) and *Butler Machine Tool Co Ltd* v *Ex-cell-o Corporation (England) Ltd* (11). His Lordship stated that in many cases the traditional analysis was out of date and that the better approach was to look at the correspondence as a whole in order to determine whether the parties had reached an agreement.

Whilst it cannot be said with certainty that the flexible approach urged by Professor Hudson, Lawton LJ and Lord Denning would necessarily be adopted by the court in the present case, it is submitted that it would be more realistic for the court to do so. My conclusion is, therefore, that the conduct of the parties precludes the formation of a binding contract.

References

1) [1968] 1 WLR 1204
2) (1818) 1 B & Ald 681
3) (1879) 4 Ex D 216
4) [1892] 2 Ch 27
5) [1983] 2 AC 74
6) [1974] 1 WLR 155
7) (1880) 5 CPD 344
8) (NZ) 1 JR (1873)
9) [1974] 4 SA 392 (c)
10) [1979] 1 WLR 294
11) [1979] 1 WLR 401

QUESTION 2

Suggested Solution

a) The first point for decision is whether in making the promise to pay £20 E had the intention to create legal relations. It has been held that in purely social and domestic arrangements there is a presumption against contractual intention, *Balfour* v *Balfour* (1), *Jones* v *Padawatton* (2), whilst in commercial or business agreements the onus is on the person asserting that no legal effect was intended, *Edwards* v *Skyways Ltd* (3). The question is one of fact in each case and is not always easy to decide as can be seen from the differing views expressed on the facts by the House of Lords in *Esso Petroleum Co Ltd* v *Commissioners of Customs and Excise* (4). Whilst the issue is not beyond doubt it is assumed that there is in the present circumstances the requisite intention.

The further question arises as to whether E's promise is supported by sufficient consideration in view of the principle that past consideration is not good consideration. This principle has been seen in operation in a number of cases, for example *Roscorla* v *Thomas* (5), *Eastwood* v *Kenyon* (6) and *Re McArdle* (7). An earlier, contrasting case, is *Lampleigh* v *Brathwait* (8). In that case the subsequent promise was coupled with the prior request to perform the activity so that the former activity amounted to good consideration for the promise.

The principle has been modified in *Re Casey's Patents, Stewart* v *Casey* (9) and the modified principle re-affirmed by the Privy Council in *Pao On* v *Lau Yiu Long* (10) and may be stated as follows: An act done before the giving of a promise can sometimes be good consideration for the promise. The act must have been done at the promisor's request; the parties must have understood that the act was to be remunerated either by a payment or the conferment of some other benefit; and the payment or the conferment of a benefit must have been legally enforceable had it been promised in advance.

If this modified principle is applied to the present facts it will appear that F's giving of the lift was done at E's request and that E's promise would, if made in advance, be legally enforceable provided there was the requisite contractual intention. What is less certain is whether it was understood by the parties that the giving of the lift was to be remunerated. This again is not beyond doubt, but it is submitted that in a business context there was the understanding that F's giving of the lift was to be remunerated either by payment or by the conferment of some benefit.

I would advise F, therefore, that E's promise to pay £20 is enforceable.

b) At common law the principle is that payment of a lesser sum does not discharge the obligation to pay the full amount contractually due, even where there has been an agreement to accept the lesser sum. This doctrine was laid down in *Pinnel's Case* (11) and affirmed by the House of Lords in *Foakes* v *Beer* (12). The rationale behind the principle is that no consideration has been furnished by the debtor for the creditor abandoning the balance of the payment due to him.

The common law has, however, been tempered by the doctrine of promissory estoppel. This doctrine was developed in the obiter dicta of Denning J (as he then was) in *Central London Property Trust Ltd* v *High Trees House Ltd* (13). Denning J derived the principle from the decision of the House of Lords in *Hughes* v *Metropolitan Railway Co* (14). It has been argued that Denning J failed to distinguish correctly contrary decisions in *Foakes* v *Beer* and *Jorden* v *Money* (15) in developing the doctrine of promissory estoppel. However, the doctrine is now well established and has been applied, inter alia, by the House of Lords in *Tool Metal Manufacturing Co Ltd* v *Tungsten Electric Co Ltd* (16) and by the Privy Council in *F A Ajayi* v *R T Briscoe (Nigeria) Ltd* (17).

The essence of the doctrine is that when one party to a contract, in the absence of fresh consideration, agrees not to enforce his rights, an equity will be raised in favour of the other party. The effect of this is that payment of a lesser sum than that contractually due may discharge the debtor's liability. If the doctrine operates in the present instance this will mean G, having paid £250, will have discharged his liability for the rent for the month of June, H by his promise being estopped from claiming the balance.

In order to determine whether the doctrine operates in G's favour certain aspects have to be considered: (i) has H made a clear and unequivocal promise; (ii) would it be inequitable to allow H to go back on that promise; (iii) has G acted on the promise sufficiently to give rise to the estoppel; (iv) is the promise extinctive or merely suspensive of H's rights? These will be considered in turn.

i) This requirement enunciated in *Woodhouse AC Israel Cocoa Ltd SA* v *Nigerian Produce Marketing Co* (18), appears to have been met.

ii) There is no evidence here of extortion or compulsion, as in *D & C Builders Ltd* v *Rees* (19) so that it would appear that it would be inequitable to allow H to go back on his promise.

iii) Has G acted on the promise? Lord Denning has maintained that all that is required to be shown is that the promisee must have been led to act differently from what he otherwise would have done and that it is not necessary to show that he acted to his detriment, *W J Alan & Co Ltd* v *El Nasr Export and Import Co* (20). This view was adopted by Robert Goff J (as he then was) in *Societe Italo-Belge* v *Palm Oils* (21) There is no clear authority for the contrary view and G may therefore be advised that it is sufficient for him to show that he has acted on the promise merely by paying the £250.

iv) Whether H's promise has an extinctive effect or is merely suspensive of his rights is uncertain in the present law. In *Ajayi* v *Briscoe* Lord Hodson stated that the promisor could resile from his promise, giving the promisee reasonable opportunity of resuming his position; and that the promise only became final and irrevocable if the promisee could not resume his position. However, this case was concerned with periodical payments, and the statement appears inappropriate to the problem under discussion. To allow H to resile from his promise would make the promise worthless.

It is therefore submitted that the promissory estoppel will operate in G's favour.

References

1) [1919] 2 KB 571
2) [1969] 1 WLR 328
3) [1964] 1 WLR 349
4) [1976] 1 WLR 1
5) (1842) 3 QB 234
6) (1840) 11 A & E 438
7) [1951] Ch 669
8) (1615) Hob 105

References (continued)

9) [1892] 1 Ch 104
10) [1980] AC 614
11) (1602) 5 Co Rep 117a
12) (1884) 9 App Cas 605
13) [1947] 1 KB 130
14) (1877) 2 App Cas 439
15) (1854) 5 HLC 185
16) [1955] 1 WLR 761
17) [1964] 1 WLR 1326
18) [1972] AC 741
19) [1966] 2 QB 617
20) [1972] 2 QB 189
21) [1982] 1 All ER 19

QUESTION 3

Suggested Solution

It is clear in this problem that the action of K's employee constitutes a breach by K of an express term of his contract with J. The question for determination is the importance of that term, that is whether the breach entitles J to treat the contract as repudiated, or whether it merely entitles J to a claim for damages.

It is therefore necessary to analyse the relative importance of contractual terms. Traditionally terms were classified as conditions and warranties, a condition being a term of such importance that any breach of it, no matter how trivial, entitled the innocent party to accept the breach and treat the contract as terminated; a warranty being a term collateral to the main purposes of the contract, the breach of which entitles the innocent party to a claim for damages but not to treat the contract as repudiated. Comparatively recently a third category of terms has been recognised by the courts – innominate or intermediate terms. In the *Hong Kong Fir Shipping* case (1) the Court of Appeal, particularly in the judgment of Diplock LJ, characterised certain contractual undertakings as being of a complex nature, which did not fit into the conventional categories of conditions and warranties. All that could be predicated of such contractual undertakings was that some breaches would and others would not deprive the innocent party of the substantial benefit of the contract. In these circumstances, in the absence of express provision in the contract, the legal consequences of the breach had to be examined in the light of the event to which the breach gave rise. The notion of the innominate term was accepted by a later Court of Appeal in *Cehave* v *Bremer* (2) and by the House of Lords in *Reardon Smith Line* v *Hansen-Tangen* (3).

What is paramount is the intention of the parties. If the parties clearly intend to classify the term as a condition the Court will give effect to that intention. What has to be examined is the contract in the light of the surrounding circumstances – *Bentsen* v *Taylor Sons & Co* (4), and the intention is to be ascertained at the time the parties entered into the agreement – *The Mihalis Angelos* (5).

Reverting to the present problem we are told that the contract describes the relevant term as a 'condition'. The use of this word is, however, not necessarily conclusive. The court will have to be satisfied that the parties intended to use the term 'condition' in the technical sense of the word; if not the court may disregard the label and examine the substance of the clause in order to determine its true nature. In *Schuler* v *Wickman Machine Tool Sales Ltd* (6) one clause of the agreement was described as a 'condition' and was the only clause bearing this description. By a 4:1 majority the House of Lords held, that in the context of the agreement as a whole the clause could not be construed as a condition. The contract as a whole between J and K is not before us so it cannot be stated categorically that the parties intended to use the word 'condition' in its technical sense. It is arguable that they did not, as the clause in question is capable of breach in a minor or trivial manner which the parties could not have envisaged as entitling J to treat the contract as repudiated.

In *Bunge Corporation* v *Tradax* (7) Lord Wilberforce made it clear that the time for determining whether a particular term was to be treated as a condition was at the time of contracting. His Lordship also recognised that the courts should not be too ready to interpret contractual clauses as conditions, but should not be reluctant to do so if the intentions of the parties, as shown by the contract, so indicated.

It is submitted that there are two provisions contained in the clause under discussion. The first is the obligation on K to perform the work with proper skill and care and the second is the obligation to ensure that the house remains habitable throughout the period of the works. It may be difficult to attribute the force of a condition to the first obligation in view of the possibility of breaches of this obligation being of a trivial nature. It should be observed that even if the obligation to perform with proper skill and care were not expressly provided for in the contract such a term would be implied. This implied term in contracts for the supply of services was recognised by the common law, see, for example *Samuels* v *Davis* (8), *Greaves & Co (Contractors) Ltd* v *Baynham Meikle and Partners* (9). This common law implied term has been enshrined in statute in the Supply of Goods and Services Act 1982 (10). It is to be noted that this statute does not specify whether this implied term is a condition or a warranty.

Whilst, for the reasons given, the court may be reluctant to construe the first obligation as a condition, it can be argued with some confidence that the requirement to maintain the house in a habitable state throughout the works was intended to be a condition, and that this intention was made manifest at the time the contract was concluded. In my view, therefore, J's later discovery that the work could have been done cheaper, whilst possibly a motivating factor in his seeking to rely on the clause, is not relevant to the question of intention.

K should therefore be advised that J is entitled to accept his (K's) breach as a repudiation of the contract which J is accordingly entitled to terminate.

References

1) [1962] 2 QB 26
2) [1976] QB 44
3) [1976] 1 WLR 989
4) [1893] 2 QB 274
5) [1971] 1 QB 164
6) [1974] AC 235
7) [1981] 1 WLR 711
8) [1943] 1 KB 526
9) [1975] 1 WLR 1095
10) section 13

QUESTION 4

Suggested Solution

a) What falls to be discussed initially here is whether a distinction can be drawn between a mistake as to identity of the contracting party and a mistake as to the attributes of that party. This distinction was made in *King's Norton Metal Co Ltd* v *Edridge, Merrett & Co Ltd* (1) where the Court of Appeal was constrained to distinguish the facts of that case from those present in the earlier case of *Cundy* v *Lindsay* (2). In the latter case a party called 'Blenkarn' disguised his letter so as to make it appear to be from a respectable firm called 'Blenkiron & Co' whom the plaintiff knew. It was held by the House of Lords that the mistake was one as to identity which rendered the contract void. In *King's Norton Metal,* on the other hand, where the rogue fraudulently misrepresented himself as the proprietor of a large business – which did not in fact exist – the mistake was held to be only one as to attributes. This rendered the contract merely voidable, not void.

In *Phillips* v *Brooks* (3) the rogue obtained goods on credit by fraudulently misrepresenting himself as a well-known titled person. The mistake here was held to be only one as to attributes, that is the creditworthiness of the rogue, and again the contract was voidable only and not void. It is difficult to distinguish this case from that of *Ingram* v *Little* (4) where the rogue in that instance obtained possession of a car from the sellers having persuaded them to accept a worthless cheque on the strength of his misrepresentation that he was some other person. In *Ingram* v *Little* the sellers were able to recover the car from an innocent third party to whom the rogue had 'sold' the car, the mistake here being regarded as one rendering the contract void.

In *Lewis* v *Averay* (5) the rogue pretended to be a well-known film actor and gave a worthless cheque in the actor's name in return for the car. The plaintiff seller only allowed the car to be taken away when the rogue produced a special admission card to a film studio to prove that he was the actor. The Court of Appeal followed *Phillips* v *Brooks* and distinguished and disapproved *Ingram* v *Little* and held that the contract was voidable only. It appears therefore that *Ingram* v *Little* is no longer to be relied on although it has not yet been overruled.

Lord Denning stated in *Lewis* v *Avery* that the distinction between a mistake as to identity and a mistake as to attributes was a distinction without a difference. His Lordship also stated that he did not accept the theory that a mistake as to identity renders a contract void. This approach is in conflict with *Cundy* v *Lindsay*, but Lord Denning expressed the view that the case would not be decided in the same way today.

Professor Glanville Williams (6) has also argued that the distinction between attributes and identity is based on a fundamental misconception. He states that what the courts have chosen to call a mistake as to identity is in fact a mistake as to attributes.

It is clear from the authorities cited that, if the distinction between attributes and identity is still valid, a mistake as to attributes does not make the contract void. What is less certain is whether this distinction can validly be made, and, if it can, the extent to which a mistake as to identity will make the contract void. This will be discussed in part (b).

b) Treitel (7) suggests that if an attribute can be used to identify a person as a particular individual there can be said to be a mistake as to identity. If a party intended to contract only with the person so identified such a mistake will render the contract void. This would explain the decision in *Lake* v *Simmons* (8). The plaintiff intended to contract with the wife of one Van der Borgh, not the woman in front of him who had falsely represented herself as such.

In the present problem the question arises whether N intended to contract with the person before him or only with the firm of Warburton & Co Ltd. The presumption is that in contracts concluded inter praesentes the party intended to contract with the person before him. What is crucial here is the time when the contract was concluded. If an agreement to sell had been reached before M misrepresented her identity N must be advised that his acceptance of the fraudulent cheque was merely a mistake as to creditworthiness, which does not render a contract void, and was, in any event, a mistake which occurred after property in the painting had passed to M. Consequently O would have acquired good title to the painting and N's only remedy would be an action for fraudulent misrepresentation against M, when and if he can find her.

If the sale is concluded concurrently with or subsequent to M's misrepresentation of her identity N might still have to be advised that the presumption operating in contracts inter praesentes would weigh against him as would the decisions in *Phillips* v *Brooks* and *Lewis* v *Avery*. In view of the conflicting authorities in this area of the law it is difficult to express an unqualified view. It is submitted, however, that the approach adopted in *Lewis* v *Avery* would also be adopted here. *Ingram* v *Little* and *Cundy* v *Lindsay* support a contrary view but the former case cannot, as has been previously said, be relied on and the latter case can be distinguished as the parties there were not inter praesentes.

References

1) (1897) 14 TLR 98
2) (1878) 3 App Cas 459
3) [1919] 2 KB 243
4) [1961] 1 QB 31
5) [1972] 1 QB 198
6) (1945) 23 Can Bar Rev 278
7) *The Law of Contract* (6th ed) pp224–5
8) [1927] AC 487

QUESTION 5

Suggested Solution

a) This quotation is an expression of the principle that the purpose of an award of damages for breach of contract is to compensate the plaintiff for the loss of bargain he has suffered as a consequence of the breach. The plaintiff must prove his loss and if he cannot do so he will be awarded only nominal damages. An alternative measure of damages to loss of bargain is to compensate the plaintiff for the wasted expenditure he has incurred as a result of the defendant's breach, see *Anglian Television Ltd* v *Reed* (1). The plaintiff has the right to choose to claim either for loss of bargain or for wasted expenditure – *CCC Films (London) Ltd* v *Impact Quadrant Films Ltd* (2), subject to the overriding requirement that the plaintiff is not to be put in a better position than he would have been if the contract had been fully performed – *C & P Haulage* v *Middleton* (3).

The award of damages for loss of bargain is subject to the limitation that the damages must not be too remote. The purpose of putting the plaintiff in the position he would have been in if the contract had been performed would, if logically pursued, give the plaintiff a complete indemnity for all loss resulting from a breach however unpredictable or improbable. It is recognised that this would be too harsh. Accordingly rules have been developed to limit the liability of the defendant to loss which the law regards as sufficiently proximate.

The modern law stems from the judgement of Alderson B in *Hadley* v *Baxendale* (4) where the rule was said to consist of two limbs. To be recoverable the damages should be such as may fairly and reasonably be considered either arising naturally, ie according to the usual course of things, from such breach of contract itself, or such as may reasonably be supposed to have been in the contemplation of both parties, at the time they made the contract, as the probable result of the breach of it.

The rule in *Hadley* v *Baxendale* was re-formulated by Asquith LJ in *Victoria Laundry (Windsor) Ltd* v *Newman Industries Ltd* (5) in the following propositions:

i) the aggrieved party is only entitled to recover loss which was at the time of the contract reasonably foreseeable as liable to result from the breach;

ii) what was reasonably foreseeable depends on the knowledge then possessed by the parties;

iii) knowledge is of two types, imputed and actual. Imputed knowledge is the knowledge that everyone, as a reasonable person, is taken to have of the ordinary course of things. Actual knowledge is knowledge which the contract-breaker actually possesses, of special circumstances outside the ordinary course of things, which make additional loss liable to result;

iv) the contract-breaker need not have actually asked himself what loss was liable to result, it is sufficient that as a reasonable man he would have done so;

v) the plaintiff need not prove that it would be foreseen that the loss would necessarily result from the breach, it was sufficient that it was a 'serious possibility' or a 'real danger'. This could be expressed as 'liable to result' or 'on the cards'.

These propositions were considered by the House of Lords in *The Heron II* (6). Whilst they were generally approved, their Lordships held that the test was not one of 'reasonable foreseeability' but one of 'reasonable contemplation' a term denoting a higher degree of probability. Their Lordships also disapproved of the colloquialism 'on the cards', and used a variety of expressions to indicate the degree of probability, including 'not unlikely', 'liable to result', 'a real danger' and 'a serious possibility'. No single formulation was adopted.

In *H Parsons (Livestock) Ltd* v *Uttley Ingham & Co Ltd* (7) Lord Denning said that different tests applied to physical (damage to person or property) and economic (deprivation of profit) loss. In the former it was sufficient if the loss was a slight possibility, in the latter it had to be shown that the loss was a serious possibility.

Scarman LJ (with whom Orr LJ agreed) rejected Lord Denning's distinction and adopted the 'serious possibility' test.

Two further points must be noted. Firstly, difficulty of assessment is no bar to an award of damages; *Chaplin* v *Hicks* (8). Secondly, damages may be awarded for distress, vexation and disappointment occasioned by a breach of contract, provided they are not too remote; see eg *Jarvis* v *Swan's Tours Ltd* (9), *Jackson* v *Horizon Holidays Ltd* (10).

b) The problem here involves the application of the rules relating to remoteness of damage previously discussed.

It is assumed that by virtue of the driver having lost his way, the hire firm are in breach of contract. It remains to consider whether, given the state of knowledge of the hire firm, the loss suffered by Bill was one that was – to use one of the expressions – a 'serious possibility'.

It is at least arguable that given that Bill was a business tycoon (a fact presumably known to the hire firm) and the type of clientele catered for by chauffeured executive cars, it was a serious possibility that loss would occur as a result of the breach, according to the usual course of things. A fortiori, if the hire firm had actual knowledge that Bill's flight to New York was for business purposes it was within their reasonable contemplation that his missing the flight, occasioned by the breach, would cause loss.

We are told that Bill missed the opportunity of obtaining the contract. It cannot, of course, be said that he would have obtained the contract had he arrived in New York as planned. This creates a difficulty in assessing damages, but this is no bar to an award. In *Chaplin* v *Hicks* (supra) the plaintiff was awarded damages for loss of the opportunity to compete in the finals of a beauty competition. The hire firm might argue that the extent of Bill's loss – relating to a multi-million dollar contract – could not have been expected. This argument cannot be sustained. In *H Parsons (Livestock) Ltd* v *Uttley Ingham & Co Ltd* Scarman LJ quoted with approval the passage in McGregor on Damages which reads:

> '... in contract as in tort, it should suffice that, if physical injury or damage is within the contemplation of the parties, recovery is not to be limited because the degree of physical injury or damage could not have been anticipated.'

Whilst this is not an area of the law in which it is possible to be certain, Bill is advised to pursue a claim for damages.

References

1) [1972] 1 QB 60
2) [1984] 3 All ER 298
3) [1983] 3 All ER 94
4) (1854) 9 Exch 341
5) [1949] 2 KB 528
6) [1969] AC 350
7) [1978] QB 791

References (continued)

8) [1911] 2 KB 786
9) [1973] 1 QB 233
10) [1975] 1 WLR 1468

QUESTION 6

Suggested Solution

Victor has made certain statements to Percy in connection with the purchase of the business. Firstly, it is necessary to discuss whether these statements are terms of the contract or mere representations. The primary consideration is the intention of the parties, *Heilbut, Symons & Co* v *Buckleton* (1), *Oscar Chess Ltd* v *Williams* (2), *Dick Bentley Productions Ltd* v *Harold Smith (Motors) Ltd* (3). The court will have regard to a number of factors; the stage at which the statements were made, whether the statements were followed by a reduction of the terms to writing, whether the person making the statements had special knowledge as compared to the other party.

It is submitted that, in view of the nature of the present statements, the court is more likely to construe them as representations rather than as contractual terms. It is, therefore, necessary to consider whether the statements amount to actionable misrepresentations. It is convenient to analyse the statements into three; the statement that the business was 'in excellent order', the assurance as to profits, and the forecast as to demand. Each statement will be considered in turn.

The statement that the business was 'in excellent order' seems, at first sight, to be what is regarded as a 'mere puff'; a simple laudatory statement made about the business will not be construed as a representation, *Dimmock* v *Hallett* (4). In the present context, however, this statement might amount to more than a mere puff, particularly in light of the warning Victor had received from his accountant.

The statement as to profits is literally correct. Whilst silence of itself does not amount to a representation, the failure to disclose the recent figures would appear to make that statement a misleading half-truth, *Dimmock* v *Hallett*. Furthermore, even if the recent figures only emerged after the statement was made, the failure to disclose the likely downturn in business will make the statement a representation, *With* v *O'Flanagan* (5). The fact that Percy did not avail himself of the opportunity of inspecting the books does not matter, *Redgrave* v *Hurd* (6).

The third statement involves a forecast of future demand. Whilst this might be regarded as a mere statement of opinion, which is not construed as a representation, *Bisset* v *Wilkinson* (7), an expression of opinion does amount to a representation where the person giving the opinion is in a position to know and could not have reasonably held that opinion, *Smith* v *Land and House Property Corporation* (8). In *Esso Petroleum Co Ltd* v *Mardon* (9) the Court of Appeal held that a forecast made by the petrol company was, in view of their special skill and knowledge, a warranty. However, it has been argued here that in the present context the statement will amount to a representation, not a contractual term. It might be suggested that, in view of Victor's illness, which necessitated the business being run by a manager, Victor's statement is only an expression of opinion, as he had at the relevant time no special knowledge. This suggestion cannot be supported; Victor is the proprietor of the firm which had received a warning from the accountant.

Accordingly, though there may be some doubt as to the first statement, it does appear that there have been representations, which are false. Provided that they induced Percy to buy the business, in the sense that they were one reason for his doing so – *Edgington* v *Fitzmaurice* (10) – an action for misrepresentation will be available to him.

We next must consider the remedies Percy could seek. This depends on whether the misrepresentations were fraudulent, negligent or innocent.

There is not sufficient evidence here to establish fraud. The essence of fraud is dishonesty, as the speech of Lord Herschell made clear in *Derry* v *Peek* (11), and the burden of proving fraud is on Percy. On the facts given it does not appear that he could discharge that burden.

For Percy to be able to claim damages the provisions of s2(1) of the Misrepresentation Act 1967 must be invoked. Section 2(1) will entitle Percy to damages unless Victor can prove that he not only believed in the truth of the representation, but had reasonable grounds for doing so, up to the time the contract was made. Despite his absence from the business through illness, it seems likely that Victor cannot discharge the burden of proof imposed on him by the Act. In particular, by ignoring, or not making himself aware of the accountant's warning, Victor is deprived of the averment that his belief is based on reasonable grounds. Support for this view can be gained from the majority judgements of the Court of Appeal in *Howard Marine & Dredging Co Ltd* v *A Ogden &*

Sons (Excavations) Ltd (12). In assessing damages the tortious measure would be employed, *Sharneyford Supplies Ltd* v *Edge* (13).

One might add that Percy would be unlikely to maintain a claim in negligence at common law; the special relationship required by *Hedley Byrne & Co Ltd* v *Heller & Partners*(14) does not appear to exist between the two parties. But, as it has been submitted that Percy has a claim under s2(1) of the 1967 Act, this is of little concern.

In addition to a claim for damages Percy will be entitled to rescission of the contract, whether the misrepresentations were negligent or innocent. They will be innocent only if Victor has proved his belief on reasonable grounds as required by s2(1). The fact that the contract between the parties has been executed is no bar to rescission, s1(b). The court has a discretion under s2(2) to award damages in lieu of rescission, but nothing here suggests why the court would exercise that discretion. Provided that there are no other bars to rescission, affirmation, delay or the acquisition of third party rights, Percy would succeed in obtaining rescission.

References

1) [1913] AC 30
2) [1957] 1 WLR 370
3) [1956] 1 WLR 623
4) (1866) LR 2 Ch App 21
5) [1936] Ch 575
6) (1818) 20 Ch D 1
7) [1927] AC 177
8) (1884) 28 Ch D 7
9) [1976] QB 801
10) (1885) 29 Ch D 459
11) (1889) 14 App Cas 337
12) [1978] QB 574
13) [1985] 1 All ER 976
14) [1964] AC 465

QUESTION 7

Suggested Solution

a) The given quotation requires an analysis of the test employed to determine whether or not a contract has been frustrated.

Prior to 1863 contractual obligations were regarded as absolute, irrespective of the change in circumstances, *Paradine* v *Jane* (1). At that date the doctrine of frustration was introduced into English law by the decision in *Taylor* v *Caldwell* (2), where it was held that a contract for the use of a music hall was frustrated when the building was destroyed by fire. This was said to rest on there being an implied term of the contract that the building should continue to exist, and on its destruction the parties were discharged of further obligations.

The courts have subsequently discarded the implied term approach in favour of the radical change in obligations tests, first propounded in the speech of Lord Radcliffe in *Davis Contractors Ltd* v *Fareham Urban District Council* (3). His Lordship said that 'frustration occurs whenever the law recognises that without default of either party a contractual obligation has become incapable of being performed because the circumstances in which performance is called for would render it a thing radically different from that which was undertaken by the contract. Non haec in foedera veni. It was not this that I promised to do'.

The principle enunciated by Viscount Radcliffe has been approved by two further decisions of the House of Lords, *National Carriers Ltd* v *Panalpina (Northern) Ltd* (4) and *The Nema* (5).

Two further points emerge from Viscount Radcliffe's speech. The first is that it is not hardship or inconvenience or material loss itself which calls the principle of frustration into play. The second is that although his Lordship referred to a contractual obligation being 'incapable of being performed' he did not mean that frustration occurs only when the contract is physically impossible of performance. Elsewhere in his speech he refers to such a change in the significance of the obligation that the thing undertaken would, if performed, be a different thing from that contracted for.

Davis v *Fareham* is itself an illustration of the first point. Delay caused by bad weather and the shortage of labour rendered the contract unprofitable for the appellants, but this did not constitute a frustrating event. Further illustration is afforded by *The Eugenia* (6) where the closure of the Suez Canal caused delay and considerable additional expense. Lord Denning emphasised the point, saying 'The fact that it has become more onerous or more expensive for one party than he thought is not sufficient to bring about a frustration. It must be more than merely more onerous or more expensive. It must be positively unjust to hold the parties bound'.

The second point, that it is not only physical impossibility that causes frustration, is illustrated by cases such as *Jackson* v *Union Marine Insurance Co Ltd* (7) and *Krell* v *Henry* (8). In both these cases physical performance was still possible, but the supervening events had rendered the nature of the contractual obligations fundamentally different.

The question is, therefore, not simply whether there has been a radical change in the circumstances, but whether there has been a radical change in the obligation. Was 'performance... fundamentally different in a commercial sense?' – *Tsakiroglou & Co Ltd* v *Noblee Thorl GmbH* (9).

b) It is submitted that the contract between Fred and Len has been frustrated. Personal incapacity such as illness has been held to be a frustrating event, *Condor* v *The Barron Knights Ltd* (10). The effect of frustration is to excuse the parties from further performance but this common law principle has been partially modified by the Law Reform (Frustrated Contracts) Act 1943.

Under s1(2) of the Act all sums paid or payable in pursuance of a frustrated contract shall be recoverable or cease to be payable. This is subject to the proviso that if the payee has incurred expense in or for the purpose of the performance of the contract, the payee may retain all or part of such sums as the court considers just up to the amount of the expenses incurred. Thus Fred can recover the £50 he has paid, subject to Len being able to retain the amount expended on the set text books.

One must next consider s1(3) of the Act. This allows Len to recover a just sum from Fred if Fred has obtained a valuable benefit under the contract prior to its being frustrated. The court must have regard to any expenses incurred by Fred, including the amount retained by Len under s1(2), and the effect of the circumstances giving rise to the frustration of the contract. The principles for calculating an award under s1(3) are contained in the judgement of Robert Goff J (as he then was) in *BP Exploration Co (Libya) Ltd* v *Hunt (No 2)* (11). It has to be shown that Len has received a valuable benefit which must be identified and valued, and this forms the upper limit of the award. The court must assess a just sum and value the benefit and award the lesser of the two.

Len has given five lessons, and as Robert Goff J indicates, a rateable part of the contract fee of, in total, £200, might provide useful evidence of the just sum. Len has given half of the lessons contracted for so that the just sum might well be £100 less the amount Len has been allowed to retain under s1(2). It might be argued that, as the balance of £150 is only payable at the end, the contract is 'entire'. But Robert Goff J stated that the fact that the contract was 'entire' should not automatically preclude an award under s1(3).

The further step required, however, is to value the benefit. Robert Goff J said that the requirement to have regard to the effect on the benefit of the frustrating event may mean in some cases that the value of the benefit is reduced to nil. This may well be the situation in the present problem, as Simon is not going to be able to take the examination for which the lessons were to prepare him.

Len should be advised, therefore, that he will be entitled to retain from the £50 he has received the amount expended on the text books, under s1(2) of the Act, but that there is some doubt as to whether he has any further claim under s1(3), the value of the benefit to Fred having been reduced to nil by virtue of the effect of the frustrating event.

References

1) (1647) Aleyn 26
2) (1863) 3 B & S 826
3) [1956] AC 696
4) [1981] AC 675
5) [1982] AC 724
6) [1964] 2 QB 226
7) (1873) LR 10 CP 125
8) [1903] 2 KB 740
9) [1962] AC 93
10) [1966] 1 WLR 87
11) [1979] 1 WLR 783

QUESTION 8

Suggested Solution

In order to decide on the effectiveness of the exclusion clause contained in the notice, it is necessary to consider three matters: whether the clause is incorporated into the contract between Tom and the Hotel; whether as a matter of construction the clause covers the incidents that occurred; and the effect, if there is an affirmative answer to both these questions, of the Unfair Contract Terms Act 1977.

Incorporation

Whether a notice displayed in premises has contractual force depends on whether the notice is in a position where it can be seen prior to, or at the time of, the conclusion of the contract. In *Alley* v *Marlborough Court Ltd* (1) the notice in a hotel bedroom purporting to exclude liability was held to be ineffective because it was only seen after the contract had been concluded. However, notice may be deemed to have been given by virtue of a course of dealings between the parties, *Spurling* v *Bradshaw* (2), *Kendall (Henry) & Sons* v *William Lillico & Sons* (3), but there must have been a consistent course of dealings, *McCutcheon* v *David MacBrayne Ltd* (4). In *Hollier* v *Rambler Motors Ltd* (5) Salmon LJ held that three or four transactions over a period of five years could not be described as a course of dealings.

The question before us does indicate a consistent course of dealings between the parties and it is, therefore, highly probable that the notice will be regarded as incorporated into the contract by this course of dealings.

It appears that the loss of Tom's car, his personal injury and the damage to his watch were all the result of negligence on the part of the Hotel and its employee. What has to be considered, therefore, is whether the notice is to be construed as excluding liability for negligence. The notice does not expressly refer to negligence, and the courts have held that where liability can arise other than by negligence then, in the absence of clear words, the exclusion clause will be held to apply to those other grounds and not to liability based on negligence, *Alderslade* v *Hendon Laundry Ltd* (6), *Gillespie Bros & Co Ltd* v *Roy Bowles Transport Ltd* (7). Liability for negligence may, however, be effectively excluded if the clause makes it clear that all damage is to be comprehended within the exclusion, from whatever cause the damage may arise. The clause in question here refers to damage 'however caused'. In *Joseph Travers & Sons Ltd* v *Cooper* (8) and *White* v *Blackmore* (9) these words have been held to be effective in excluding liability for negligence.

Having concluded that the notice has been incorporated into the contract and that it does, as a matter of construction, exclude liability for negligence, it remains to consider the effect of the Unfair Contract Terms Act 1977.

Under s 2(1) of the Act the purported exclusion of liability for personal injury resulting from negligence is rendered totally ineffective. It can be assumed that leaving the corridor in a highly polished state constitutes negligence on the part of the Hotel, and the Hotel will, in consequence, be liable to Tom for the personal injury he has sustained.

The damage caused to Tom's wristwatch falls within the ambit of s 2(2) of the Act which requires the notice, to be effective, to satisfy the reasonableness test. (It should be noted that Tom's awareness of the notice does not of itself indicate his voluntary acceptance of any risk – s 2(3) of the Act). Under s 11(1) of the Act the requirement of reasonableness is that the notice shall be a fair and reasonable one having regard to the circumstances which were, or ought reasonably to have been, known to or in the contemplation of the parties at the time the contract was made. By virtue of s 11(5) of the Act the onus of proving that the exclusion clause satisfies the reasonableness test is on the Hotel.

The reasonableness test (imposed by an enactment now superseded by the Unfair Contract Terms Act) was considered by the House of Lords in *George Mitchell (Chesterfield) Ltd* v *Finney Lock Seeds Ltd* (10) where the limitation clause was held not to be reasonable since the practice of the sellers had been not to rely on the clause in the past but to negotiate settlements of claims. The decision in *George Mitchell* does not provide a great deal of assistance in the present problem. It is submitted that the approach to be adopted here is that indicated by Lord Wilberforce in *Photo Productions Ltd* v *Securicor Transport Ltd* (11) where his Lordship said that in commercial matters, when the parties are not of unequal bargaining power, and when risks are normally borne by insurance, the parties should be left to apportion the risks as they think fit. This approach was adopted by Staughton J in applying the reasonableness test in *Stag Line Ltd* v *Tyne Shiprepair Group Ltd* (12).

I would conclude that the exclusion clause satisfies the reasonableness test so as to exclude the Hotel from liability for the loss of Tom's wristwatch.

With regard to the theft of Tom's car, two matters arise for consideration, the liability of the Hotel itself and the liability of the porter. For the reasons previously given I would advise Tom that the Hotel will be able to rely on the exclusion clause. No distinction can be drawn, in principle, between the loss of the wristwatch and the loss of the car.

The final point to be considered is the liability of the porter for his negligent acts. The clause purports to exclude the liability of employees, and the question is whether the rules of privity of contract will prevent the porter from relying on the clause. It is submitted that the decision in *Adler* v *Dickson* (13) and the speeches of the majority in *Scruttons Ltd* v *Midland Silicones Ltd* (14) would preclude the porter from relying on the clause. There are special circumstances in which a third party can rely on the benefit of an exclusion clause as appear from the two Privy Council decisions in *New Zealand Shipping Co Ltd* v *Satterthwaite (The Eurymedon)* (15) and *Port Jackson Stevedoring Ltd* v *Salmond & Spraggon Ltd (The New York Star)* (16).

The special circumstances were recently considered in *Southern Water Authority* v *Carey* (17). It would have to be established, inter alia, that the Hotel had authority from the employee that the clause should also apply to him at the time it contracted with Tom and that it could be shown that consideration had moved from the employee. There is no evidence that these requirements have been met.

References

1) [1949] 1 KB 532
2) [1956] 1 WLR 461
3) [1969] 2 AC 31
4) [1964] 1 WLR 125
5) [1972] 2 QB 71
6) [1945] KB 189
7) [1973] QB 400
8) [1915] 1 KB 73
9) [1972] 2 QB 651
10) [1983] 2 All ER 737
11) [1980] AC 827
12) [1984] 2 Lloyd's Rep 211
13) [1955] 1 QB 158
14) [1962] AC 446

References (continued)

15) [1975] AC 154
16) [1980] 1 WLR 138
17) [1985] 2 All ER 1077

QUESTION 9

Suggested Solution

The first principle which Treitel mentions is given effect to by the general common law rule that an infant is not bound by certain contracts. The common law, in this respect, is reinforced by the Infants Relief Act 1874. The second principle finds expression in the rules that certain contracts with infants are valid, others are merely voidable at the instance of the infant, and an infant may incur some liability in tort, quasi-contract and in equity. To reconcile these two principles does create some problems for the law, though perhaps on a smaller scale than prior to 1969, when the Family Reform Act of that year reduced the age of majority from 21 to 18.

Valid contracts

An infant is bound by contracts for necessaries. Necessaries include goods and services which are fit to maintain the infant in the station of life to which he is accustomed, *Peters* v *Fleming* (1). Necessary goods are defined by s3(3) Sale of Goods Act 1979 as 'goods suitable to the condition in life of the minor ... and to his actual requirements at the time of sale and delivery.' The onus of proof is on the supplier to show that the goods are capable of being necessaries, *Ryder* v *Wombwell* (2) and that the goods purchased actually were necessary at the time of purchase, *Nash* v *Inman* (3).

It is not entirely clear whether an infant is bound by an executory contract for necessary goods. Section 3(2) of the Sale of Goods Act provides that an infant must pay a reasonable price for 'necessaries sold and delivered'. And necessaries are defined in s 3(3) in relation to the time of sale and delivery. Is the infant liable if the goods have been sold, but not yet delivered? The answer depends on whether the infant is liable *re,* that is because he has been supplied, or *consensu,* that is because he has contracted. The wording of s 3 suggests that the infant is liable *re,* because he has been supplied. Conflicting views were expressed in *Nash* v *Inman.* Fletcher Moulton LJ said that the infant was liable because he had been supplied, not because he had contracted. Buckley LJ held, however, that the infant was liable because he had contracted. In *Roberts* v *Gray* (4) it was held that an infant was bound by an executory contract for services and education and it is difficult to see how a valid distinction can be drawn between goods and services on this point.

An infant cannot be made liable on a loan to him to purchase necessaries, s1 Infants Relief Act, but if the loan is actually spent on necessaries equity will allow recovery of the money so spent, *Marlow* v *Pitfield* (5).

Contracts for service, apprenticeship and education are binding on the infant if the contract as a whole is for his benefit, even if certain clauses in it are harsh, *Clements* v *L & NW Railway* (6). In *De Francesco* v *Barnum* (7) the infant was not bound because the overriding effect of the contract was held to be oppressive. The binding effect of service contracts has been extended to contracts for the exercise of a profession, *Doyle* v *White City Stadium* (8), *Chaplin* v *Leslie Frewin (Publishers) Ltd* (9), *Denmark Productions Ltd* v *Boscobel Productions Ltd* (10). The law distinguishes between an infant who earns his living by the exercise of a profession and one who earns his living by trading, because in the latter case he risks his capital. 'The law will not suffer him to trade, which may be his undoing' – *Whywall* v *Campion* (11).

Voidable contracts

Certain contracts subsist unless and until avoided. In the case of infants' voidable contracts only the infant may avoid them. The kinds of contract that are voidable at the instance of the infant are:

i) contracts concerning real property;

ii) contracts involving shares in companies;

iii) partnership agreements; and

iv) marriage settlements.

These contracts would not be considered as for necessaries, but to consider them void might well work injustice to the other party, as they involve reciprocal liability extending over a period of time.

The rules relating to infants' voidable contracts are (a) that he must repudiate before or within a reasonable time of attaining majority; and (b) the effect of repudiation is that he is relieved of obligations arising after the time of repudiation, but remains bound to meet obligations which have already arisen and cannot recover money paid prior to that time, *Steinberg* v *Scala (Leeds) Ltd* (12).

Void contracts

Section 1 of the Infants Relief Act provides that contracts entered into by infants for 'the repayment of money lent or to be lent' or for 'goods supplied or to be supplied (other than ... necessaries)' and 'all accounts stated' shall be 'absolutely void'.

The effect of the words 'absolutely void' is not entirely clear. Generally money paid under a void contract can be recovered, but in *Valentini* v *Canali* (13) an infant was denied recovery and in *Pearce* v *Brain* (14) it was held that an infant plaintiff could not recover unless there had been a total failure of consideration. Normally, too, property does not pass under a void contract, but in *Stock* v *Wilson* (15) Lush J expressed the view, *obiter* that property in non-necessary goods obtained by an infant is passed on delivery.

Section 2 of the Infants Relief Act also provides that fresh promises made after majority do not render a 'debt' contracted during infancy actionable, nor does any ratification of any promise or contract made during infancy.

Liability of infants in tort

An infant cannot be sued in tort for an act which was within the contemplation of the void contract, *Jennings* v *Rundall* (16). If, however, the wrongful act is of a kind not contemplated by the contract, the infant may be exposed to tortious liability, *Burnard* v *Haggis* (17).

Liability of infants in equity

The court may have power to order restitution against the infant where the infant still has the property in his possession.

In *Stocks* v *Wilson* where the infant misrepresented his age to obtain property he was held liable to account for the proceeds of the sale of the property by him to a third party. The infant cannot, however, be held to account for money which he has dissipated.

Proposed reforms

In 1967 the Latey Committee on the Age of Majority (18) recommended that the Infants Relief Act should be totally repealed. It proposed that all contracts should be unenforceable against an infant, subject to the infant being liable to account to the adult party for any money, goods or other benefit received. These proposals have not been implemented.

The Law Commission suggested in 1982 (19) that infants should have full contractual capacity at the age of sixteen. Under that age an infant should not be liable on, but able to enforce his contracts with an adult party. The adult party should be entitled to recover any property transferred to an infant under sixteen and which has not been paid for. But the adult party should not be entitled to recover the price, or money lent or to assert any other remedy to enforce the contract.

References

1) (1840) 6 M & W 42
2) (1869) LR 4 Ex 32
3) [1908] 2 KB 1
4) [1914] 1 KB 520
5) (1719) 1 P Wms 558
6) [1894] 2 QB 482
7) (1889) 43 Ch D 165
8) [1935] 1 KB 110
9) [1966] Ch 71
10) [1969] 1 QB 699
11) (1738) 2 Stra 1083
12) [1923] 2 Ch 452
13) (1889) 24 QBD 166
14) [1929] 2 KB 310
15) [1913] 2 KB 235
16) (1799) 8 TR 335
17) (1863) 14 CB 45
18) Cmnd 3342
19) Law Commission Working Paper No 81 (1982)

UNIVERSITY OF LONDON
INTERMEDIATE EXAMINATION IN LAWS 1987
for External Students

ELEMENTS OF THE LAW OF CONTRACT

Tuesday, 9 June: 10.00 am to 1.00 pm

Answer *FIVE* of the following NINE questions.

1 Bob owns a stamp shop in Muncaster High Street. On Monday he places an item in the advertisement column of the Muncaster Evening Gazette. 'Utopian Penny Red Stamp, one only, £750 or nearest offer.'

Later that day, Alan, a stamp collector, telephones Bob and says, 'The Utopian Red for sale, I'll take it for £700.' Bob replies, 'I cannot accept less than £725 but I will not sell it to anyone else before Saturday. Let me have a reply by Friday if you want it.' Alan says 'That is kind of you. Remind me to buy you a drink when I see you.'

On Wednesday Alan telephones Bob and leaves a message on his answering machine stating 'I accept your offer.' Unfortunately Bob's infant son later presses a button on the machine which erases the message before Bob listens to the recording. Later that day Bob sells the stamp to Cedric for £750.

On Thursday Alan meets Cedric's aged mother who tells him that she has seen Cedric's nine year old son who told her that his father was very excited at having acquired a Utopian Penny red from a High Street dealer.

Alan rushes home and posts a letter to Bob confirming the message which he had left on the machine. On the same day Bob writes to Alan withdrawing his offer.

On Friday morning Alan receives Bob's letter and at lunchtime Bob receives Alan's letter.

Advise Alan.

2 a) Consider to what extent, if any, a person provides consideration for a promise by doing or promising to do what he was already contractually bound to do.

b) Albert rents a caravan from Bernard. Albert's wife, Wendy, is subsequently injured in a road accident and has to give up work. After a discussion between them Bernard promises Albert that he will accept half rent until Wendy is able to go back to work. Albert pays half rent for the next twelve months but is then advised that Wendy will never be able to work again. On learning this Bernard tells Albert that he wants full rent from now and also the balance of the past twelve month's rent.

Advise Albert. How would your advice differ, if at all, if Wendy had recently received £100,000 compensation for her injuries?

3 'The nineteenth century distinction between "conditions" and "warranties" has given way to a more flexible test.' (Anson's *Law of Contract*).

Consider in the light of the existing case law.

4 Victor advertises a second hand motorcycle in his sales showroom. 'BMW. 1984. Excellent condition. 6,000 miles. One Previous owner. £2000 only. Suitable for racing.' Percy goes to see it. Victor says that 'It is in fine condition but have it independently examined if you wish.' Percy says that that will not be necessary because he is content to rely on Victor's fine reputation. He then buys the motorcycle for £2,000.

A year later he discovers that the motorcycle had had three previous owners, had done 60,000 miles and was worth only £1,000 at the time of the sale. Furthermore it has proved most unsuitable for racing.

Advise Percy.

5 a) 'Mistake is said to negative consent when it leads to a misunderstanding between the parties, so that they are at cross purposes ... It cannot be too strongly emphasised that in this type of case a mistake "will not normally affect the validity of the contract at all" the mistake will only impair the validity of the contract in a number of somewhat exceptional situations.' (Treitel).

Explain and illustrate the above passage with reference to the relevant case law.

b) A computer firm with whom he has had previous dealings writes to 'Professor A Higgins, University of Life' offering a consultancy contract worth £5,000. The letter is forwarded to professor Albert Higgins in the Faculty of Science. In fact the firm had meant it to go to Professor Andrew Higgins in the Faculty of Technology. Albert Higgins replies accepting the offer but the firm are now refusing to honour it.

Advise him.

6 Phil, an old age pensioner with poor eyesight, decides to book a touring holiday for himself and his wife in the Highlands and Islands of Scotland with 'Countryside Tours', a company which specialises in cheap holidays for old people. He had seen the tour advertised in a brochure.

As part of the deal Phil receives a wallet full of accommodation and travel vouchers. On the back of each document in small print are the terms (which are also displayed in the office where Phil booked the holiday) including the following clauses –

a) Neither the company nor its employees or agents shall be liable for negligent acts or omissions occasioning injury to customers or damage to or loss of their property.

b) Any liability of the Company, its employees or agents shall be limited to £50.

One afternoon the coach in which Phil and his wife are travelling crashes when the driver takes a sharp bend at high speed whilst racing with a driver from another firm. Phil suffers a broken leg and spends the remainder of the holiday in hospital whilst his wife who suffers from shock as a consequence of the accident has to return home immediately. Phil's expensive cine-camera is also damaged beyond repair.

Advise Phil and his wife.

7 Lord Blessers, who wishes to celebrate his daughter's wedding in style, arranges an open air pop concert in Blessers Park, in the county of Loamshire. On 1st February he engages a famous group 'The Wild Things' to appear for £5,000. He is obliged to pay them £1,000 immediately, the balance to be payable on 1 July, the day of the concert. On 1 March he engages a catering firm 'Eatwell' to provide 500 lunches in a marquee in Blessers Park for £10,000, payable on 1 July. On June 1 foot and mouth disease, which has been affecting neighbouring counties for the previous six months, breaks out in Loamshire. The disease cannot be contracted by human beings but can be spread by them. The Minister of Agriculture appeals to residents of Loamshire, on a 'voluntary basis', to cancel any outdoor events.

Lord Blessers immediately cancels the celebrations and informs the group and the caterers that their services are no longer required. The group has spent considerable sums of money setting up an elaborate stage whilst the caterers have incurred considerable expense in preparations.

Advise 'The Wild Things' and 'Eatwell'.

How would your advice differ, if at all, if the bride had been killed in an accident a week before her wedding day?

8 a) 'Damages cannot, in principle, be recovered in a contractual action for hurt feelings, disappointment or injury to reputation.'

Discuss.

b) A Ltd employ B Ltd to build a multi-purpose sports complex. B Ltd engage sub-contractors, C Ltd, who use cement which turns out to be highly unsuitable for the purpose for which it is used. Soon after completion and occupation of the building cracks begin to appear. The complex has to close for expensive repairs and a lot of revenue is lost. A Ltd had also put in a bid, which has to be withdrawn, to host the World Badminton Championships which would have produced large amounts of revenue.

Advise A Ltd.

9 'The doctrine of restraint of trade is one to be applied to factual situations with a broad and flexible rule of reason.' (Lord Wilberforce)

Explain the factual situations to which the doctrine has been applied and the principles upon which it operates.

QUESTION 1

Suggested Solution

In advising Alan, one must carefully analyse the various actions of and communications passing between the parties in order to determine whether at any stage he entered into a contract with Bob to buy the stamp in question.

The first material event was Bob's placing of an advertisement in the Gazette. Although there is no reason in principle why an advertisement should not constitute a contractual offer, this will normally only be so in the case of unilateral contracts (eg *Carlill* v *Carbolic Smoke Ball Co* (1)). Since the envisaged contract here is bilateral, a court would construe Bob's advertisement as being an invitation to treat only: *Partridge* v *Crittenden* (2).

Alan's telephone reply, although couched in terms of an acceptance, can only be offer as there has been no prior offer capable of being accepted. A statement can be an offer although expressed as an acceptance: *Bigg* v *Boyd Gibbins Ltd* (3).

Alan's offer is not accepted by Bob. The latter's reply, however, gives rise to a problem of construction: it could be regarded as a rejection and counter offer (*Hyde* v *Wrench* (4) and *Butler Machine Tool* v *Ex-cell-o Corp* (5)) or a rejection together with a statement as to price (similar to *Harvey* v *Facey* (6)). It is submitted that the last part of Bob's reply, giving Alan until Friday to respond, indicates that the first construction is correct.

Bob has promised to keep his counter offer open until Friday. It is to be noted that he is under no obligation so to do. A gratuitous promise to keep an offer open for a fixed period time is not binding on the offeror, *Routledge* v *Grant* (7), and he can revoke the offer at any time. The only way an offer may be irrevocable for a fixed time is if the offeree furnishes consideration for the offeror's promise not to revoke, but Alan has not done so. Alan's promise to buy Bob a drink is a consequence of Bob's promise to keep the offer open; it was not requested by him nor was it given in return for Bob's promise in the contractual sense: *Combe* v *Combe* (8).

Next Alan dictates a message of acceptance on Bob's answering machine on Wednesday. The general rule is that an acceptance is ineffective unless and until communicated to the offeror: *Holwell*

Securities Ltd v *Hughes* (9). Although different principles apply to acceptance by letter or telegram (to be dealt with below), in *Entores* v *Miles Far East Corp* (10), approved in *Brinkibon* v *Stahag Stahl* (11), the Court of Appeal held that an acceptance by telephone or telex is only effective when received.

This principle was formulated on the proposition that telephones and telexes are instantaneous means of communication. That is obviously not the case where an acceptance is left on an answering machine. It is submitted, though, that there is no warrant for extending the postal acceptance rule to messages left on answering machines and that Alan's acceptance would only be effective when heard by Bob.

Due to the activities of Bob's son, he never heard it. Although one might refer to dicta in *Entores*, and also the *The Brimnes* (12), as indicating that where one party's failure to receive communication is due to his own default, he is to be treated as having received it, it is doubtful whether the infant's activities can be placed in this class.

Thus when Bob sells the stamps to Cedric, and also when Alan hears news of Cedric's excitement, Alan has not accepted Bob's offer. Equally, though, Bob has not revoked it, since revocation of an offer must be communicated: *Byrne* v *Van Tienhoven* (13).

In *Dickinson* v *Dodds* (14) it appears to have been held either that sale of the subject matter of the offer, or at any rate communication of the fact of the sale by a third party to the offeree operates to revoke the offer. Whatever the true ratio of that case, which has been much criticised, it is very unlikely that a court would hold that the information given to Alan by Cedric's mother acquired from Cedric's son constituted revocation of Bob's offer. Although Alan may have suspected it was the same stamp, he could not have known it was, nor even that the information was strictly correct.

Bob's offer is thus still capable of acceptance when Alan posts his letter. The key issue now is whether the postal acceptance rule applies. If it does, a contract was concluded when Alan posted his letter: *Adams* v *Lindsell* (15), *Household Insurance* v *Grant* (16) and *Henthorn* v *Fraser* (17). Conversely it is settled law that Bob's letter of revocation is effective only when received by Alan: *Byrne* v *Van Tienhoven*.

The postal acceptance rule does not invariably apply. It is a rule of convenience which may (inter alia) be ousted by contrary stipulation: *Holwell* v *Hughes*. Although the language used by Bob was not totally clear, the words 'Let me have a reply by Friday' suggest that to be effective the acceptance must be received by him.

On this interpretation, as Alan's letter of acceptance arrived after Bob's letter of revocation, it is submitted that no contract was concluded.

One's advice to Alan is, therefore, that he has no claim.

References

1) [1893] 1 QB 256
2) [1968] 1 WLR 1204
3) [1971] 1 WLR 913
4) (1840) 3 Beav 334
5) [1979] 1 WLR 401
6) [1893] AC 552
7) (1828) 4 Bing 653
8) [1951] 2 KB 215
9) [1974] 1 WLR 155
10) [1955] 2 QB 327
11) [1983] 2 AC 34
12) [1975] QB 929
13) (1880) 5 CPD 344
14) (1876) 2 Ch D 463
15) (1818) 1 B & Ald 681
16) (1879) 4 Ex D 216
17) [1892] 2 Ch 27

QUESTION 2 (a)

Suggested Solution

Two different situations must be considered here, namely:

i) where the contractual duty in question is owed to the promisor;

ii) where such duty is owed not to the promisor but to a third party.

As to (i), although there are relatively few cases on the topic and none of very high authority, the position at present is that the performance or promise of performance of an existing contractual duty owed to the promisor is not good consideration. Thus in *Stilk* v *Myrick* (1) sailors who were promised a share of the wages of two deserters for working the ship home failed in an action brought on that promise. Because they were already contractually bound to work her home, they furnished no consideration for the promise. Conversely in *Hartley* v *Ponsonby* (2) the level of desertions was so high that the sailors would have been justified in refusing to work further. By remaining at their posts, they therefore did more than their existing contractual duty and succeeded in an action on a promise to pay them additional remuneration. This distinction between merely doing that which one is bound to do by contract with the promisor, and doing over and above one's duty, was accepted and applied more recently by Mocatta J in *The Atlantic Baron* (3).

As to (ii), three nineteenth century cases, *Shadwell* v *Shadwell* (4), *Scotson* v *Pegg* (5) and *Chichester* v *Cobb* (6) suggested (without definitively deciding) that the performance or promise of performance of an existing contractual duty owed to a third party could be good consideration. Two recent decisions of the Privy Council, *New Zealand Shipping Co* v *AM Satterthwaite* (7) and *Pao On* v *Lau Yiu* (8) have stated clearly and unequivocally that this is indeed the law. Although neither is strictly binding in England, it is almost inconceivable that the English court would not adopt this principle. In a third party case, therefore, the performance or promise of performance of the existing duty is sufficient on its own and there is no need to look for some additional element of consideration over and above the duty itself.

In *Ward* v *Byham* (9) and *Williams* v *Williams* (10), Denning LJ (as he then was) suggested a more radical approach. His Lordship suggested that the performance of an existing duty (of whatever type) should be good consideration providing there was nothing in the transaction contrary to the public interest: his Lordship was perhaps thinking of duress, improper pressure or unfair bargaining being involved. Although this view has attracted academic support, it has not yet been adopted by the courts and it is thus still necessary to distinguish (in cases involving existing contractual duties) between the two and three party cases.

References

1) (1809) 2 Camp 317
2) (1857) 7 E & B 872
3) [1979] QB 705
4) (1860) 9 CB 159
5) (1861) 6 H & N 293
6) (1866) 14 LT 433
7) [1975] AC 154
8) [1980] AC 614
9) [1956] 1 WLR 496
10) [1957] 1 WLR 148

QUESTION 2 (b)

Suggested Solution

In advising Albert one must consider the principles governing discharge of a debtor when he makes part payment only and whether the doctrine of promissory estoppel may afford him a defence as to all or part of Bernard's claim.

The general rule is that a creditor who promises to accept a lesser sum in satisfaction of a larger debt can subsequently insist on the balance being paid unless the debtor has furnished consideration for that promise: *Pinnel's Case* (1) and *Foakes* v *Beer* (2). Prima facie, Bernard can therefore recover the balance of the past twelve month's rent and insist on the full amount hereafter.

However the doctrine of promissory estoppel can provide a good defence to a debtor in Albert's position in certain cases. This doctrine, which owes its existence to certain obiter remarks of Denning J. (as he then was) in *Central London Property Trust* v *High Trees House* (3), relying on the decision of the House of Lords in *Hughes* v *Metropolitan Railway Co* (4), is an important exception to the general rule above stated. For this to apply, a number of conditions must be satisfied.

First, there must be a promise by the creditor (Bernard) which is intended to affect the parties' legal relations and which is not a mere concession or indulgence: *High Trees* and *Woodhouse* v *Nigerian Produce Marketing* (5). It is submitted that this condition is satisfied.

Secondly, the debtor (Albert) must act on the promise. Although certain cases, eg *Ajayi* v *RT Briscoe* (6), suggest that the debtor must alter his position to his detriment (the classic equitable requirement for estoppel), the preponderance of authority indicates that this is not necessary here. There was no detriment present in *High Trees* and in *Alan* v *El Nasr* (7). Lord Denning disclaimed it as an element of promissory estoppel, saying it was sufficient if the debtor acted on the promise by paying the lesser sum. Robert Goff J. (as he then was) adopted the same view in *Societe Italo-Belge* v *Palm Oils* (8). Thus by paying the lower rent, Albert did act on Bernard's promise.

Thirdly, it must be inequitable for the creditor (Bernard) to go back on his promise. There are two aspects to this third condition. In the first place, the creditor's promise must not have been extracted by threats or coercion by the debtor, as happened in *D & C Builders* v *Rees* (9). There is no evidence of that here. Next, it must be borne in mind that in certain cases the courts have allowed a debtor to resile from his promise and to insist on his full contractual rights in future: *Tungsten Electric* v *Tool Metal* (10) and *Ajayi* v *Briscoe.*

As to the balance of the rent over the last twelve months, it is submitted (for the reasons given in *High Trees*) that it would be inequitable for Bernard to go back on his promise. There is no reason for believing that he intended to suspend payment of the balance, he intended to forego it altogether.

As to the future payments, however, Albert's case is less strong. Bernard agreed to accept half rent until Wendy was able to go back to work, both sides believing that at some stage she would be able to return. That belief was unfounded. It would be a harsh conclusion to draw that as a result of that mistaken belief, Bernard is bound to accept half rent for the remainder of the lease. A court would be likely to hold that he would insist on being paid the full rent on giving reasonable notice.

If Wendy received £100,000 compensation, this would obviously make Bernard's claim to the balance of the past rent more difficult to resist. It was a promise induced by Albert and Wendy's poor financial circumstances. If their financial position were to be improved so dramatically a court might well conclude that it would not be inequitable for Bernard to insist on both the full rent henceforth and to recover the balance of past payments.

References

1) (1602) 5 Co Rep 117a
2) (1884) 9 App Cas 605
3) [1947] KB 130
4) (1877) 2 App Cas 439
5) [1972] AC 741
6) [1964] 1 WLR 1326
7) [1972] 2 QB 189
8) [1982] 1 All ER 19
9) [1966] 2 QB 617
10) [1955] 1 WLR 761

QUESTION 3

Suggested Solution

First it is necessary to define the subject matter of this answer. The distinction referred to between conditions and warranties is the apparent approach of nineteenth century contract lawyers to the classification of contractual terms. They appear generally (the reason for their qualification is given later in this answer) to have regarded the categories of conditions and warranties as being exhaustive: a contractual term had to be either one or the other. It is clear now, however, that English law recognises not two but three different types of terms: conditions, warranties and innominate terms (sometimes called intermediate stipulations).

A condition may be defined as a term, any breach of which entitles the innocent party not only to recover damages but also to terminate the contract if he so chooses, irrespective of the consequences of the breach. The right to terminate, which is an option not an obligation, arises because of the nature of the term broken, not because of the consequences which flow from the breach: *Hong Kong Fir Shipping* v *Kawasaki Kisen Kaisha* (1); *Bunge* v *Tradax* (2); and *Lombard North Central* v *Butterworth* (3).

An innominate term is a term, a breach of which entitles the innocent party to recover damages and may, in addition, entitle him to terminate the contract. The right to terminate is not always available, as with a condition, but only where the actual and prospective consequences of the breach are such as to deprive the innocent party of substantially the whole of the benefit of the consideration he bargained to receive under the contract (in short, where the breach goes to the root of the contract): *Hong Kong Fir Shipping*. Thus in the case of an innominate term, the existence of the right to terminate depends upon the severity of the consequences of the breach.

A warranty is a term, any breach of which is remediable in damages only: *Bettini* v *Gye* (4). It would appear that no matter how serious the breach or its consequences, if the term is broken is only a warranty then there is never a right to terminate the contract. Although this may seem harsh at first sight, to hold otherwise would so blur the distinction between innominate terms and warranties as to render it unworkable.

The reason for the qualifying remarks at the beginning of this answer can now be stated. Although this three-fold classification of contractual terms has been accepted and applied in practice since *Hong Kong Fir* in 1962, it has been suggested in some of the cases that innominate terms were recognised in earlier decisions in the twentieth century and in the nineteenth century too. The Court of Appeal made this point very forcibly in *Cehave* v *Bremer* (5) and in *Bunge* v *Tradax* the House of Lords expressed similar views. For example Lord Searman spoke of innominate terms being 'rediscovered' in *Hong Kong Fir* but of always having been part of English law.

If these views be accepted, then Anson is wrong to suggest that a two-fold classification only existed in the last century. However it is fair to say that even if innominate terms were known to English law before 1962, they were largely (though perhaps not entirely) overlooked by both judges and academics alike.

The three-fold classification is in any event now established. Taken out of context, though, Anson's proposition could be read as meaning that the classification of terms (albeit into three rather than two categories) is no longer important. It is respectfully submitted that this is not so, nor did the editor of Anson intend so to suggest.

The classification of terms is important. For the parties to know their legal rights and liabilities, the nature of the term is crucial, particularly as regards the availability or otherwise of the rights of termination. Further, the character of all terms is ascertainable at the moment the contract is concluded. Nothing that happens after its formation can alter the status of a term, although in the case of an innominate term it will determine the availability of the right of termination. To hold otherwise would lead to unacceptable uncertainty: a contract term cannot have a status capable of changing from one day to the next.

The flexibility to which Anson refers is introduced into the law by the innominate term. Instead of saying that the innocent can, in the case of a condition, always terminate, or in the case of warranty, never terminate is manifestly inflexible. Innominate terms allow the courts to permit termination where the circumstances justify it and the consequences are sufficiently serious. It is for this reason that innominate terms were regarded with obvious favour in cases such as *Hong Kong Fir; Cehave* v *Bremer; Schuler* v *Wickman Machine Tool* (6) and *Reardon Smith* v *Hansen-Tangen* (7).

Nevertheless innominate terms are only one of the three categories and the other two cannot be ignored. It may be, for example, that the term in question is expressly designated a condition as a warranty by statute, such as the Sale of Goods Act 1979, or has already been judicially classified, as was the case in *The Mihalis Angelos* (8). Further, it is open to the parties themselves expressly to classify the term, in which case providing their intention is clear the courts will give effect to it: *The Chikuma* (9) and *Lombard North Central*. Lastly the courts may be of the view that the parties must have intended the term to be a condition, even though they did not bother so to call it. The most obvious examples here are stipulations as to time in mercantile contracts: *United Scientific Holdings* v *Burnley BC* (10) and *Bunge* v *Tradax*. In all these cases, there is no flexibility. The right to terminate for breach (or not, in the case of warranty) follows on from the classification of the term.

In conclusion, whilst Anson is right to suggest that there is now greater flexibility in this area of the law, the distinction between the different types of contractual terms remains of considerable importance.

References

1) [1962] 2 QB 26
2) [1981] 1 WLR 711
3) [1987] 1 All ER 267
4) (1876) 1 QBD 183
5) [1976] QB 44
6) [1974] AC 235
7) [1976] 1 WLR 989
8) [1971] 1 QB 164
9) [1981] 1 WLR 314
10) [1978] AC 904

QUESTION 4

Suggested Solution

Percy has a number of complaints arising out of the advertisement he read before going to see and then purchasing the motorcycle. One must consider whether he has any claims for (a) breach of contract and (b) misrepresentation.

First one must consider whether any of the statements made by Victor in his advertisement were incorporated as terms of the contract. The test is one of contractual intention, *Heilbut, Symons & Co* v *Buckleton* (1), namely would the reasonable man have understood that the maker of the statement intended to be contractually bound?

Although the courts often regard laudatory pre-contractual statements as having no contractual effect, the position may be different where the maker of the statement is a tradesman carrying on his business. In *Dick Bentley* v *Harold Smith Motors* (2) the Court of Appeal held that a dealer's pre-contractual statement as to a car's recorded mileage did constitute a term of the contract. If that case were to be followed here, Percy could well have claims for breach of contract arising out of Victor's statements as to the motorcycle's mileage and number of previous owners. He would recover damages calculated according to the contractual loss of bargain measure, i.e. to put him in the position he would have been in had the statements been true (*Robinson* v *Harman* (3) and *Radford* v *De Froberville* (4)). In money terms, this would be the difference in value between a BMW 1984 motorcycle as described and the motorcycle which he in fact purchased.

Next one must consider the Sale of Goods Act 1979. Although this probably was a sale by description, it is submitted that Victor was not in breach of the condition implied into the contract by s13(1) of the 1979 Act that the goods should correspond with the description: Percy contracted for and got a BMW 1984 model motorcycle. Further, there is no suggestion that it was not of merchantable quality, contrary to s14(2) of the 1979 Act, since Percy apparently used the machine for a year.

There is more scope for argument concerning s14(3) of the 1979 Act, namely fitness for purpose. Victor advertised the motorcycle as being suitable for racing, but it has proved not to be so. If Percy, either expressly or by implication, made known to Victor that he was buying it for the purpose of racing, then Victor would be in breach of this condition. It is probably too late for Percy now to reject the goods, as he will be deemed to have accepted them under s35(1) of the 1979 Act. Again, however, he would be entitled to recover damages calculated according to the contract loss of bargain measure.

Aside from Percy's contractual remedies, one must consider possible claims for misrepresentation. Although the relevant statements appear to have been in printed form rather than being made orally, this matters not. Also, since the passing of the Misrepresentation Act 1967, it matters not either that any or all of the statements were incorporated as terms of the contract, or that the contract has been executed (s1 of that Act).

It is submitted that Victor's statements as to mileage, previous owners and suitability for racing constitute actionable misrepresentations. Both were false statements of facts addressed to potential purchasers (ie a class of persons of whom Percy was a member) and seem to have induced him to enter into the contract; at least they induced him to go and see the motorcycle. The test as to inducement is a fairly relaxed one. In *Edgington* v *Fitzmaurice* (5) it was held to be sufficient that the misrepresentation was a reason for the representee having entered into the contract. Further, it matters not that Percy did not have the motorcycle independently examined. *Redgrave* v *Hurd* (6) is authority that the representee is under no duty to check the accuracy of the representator's statements.

Conversely there is nothing to indicate that Victor was incorrect in advertising the motorcycle as a 1984 model, and his description of it as being in excellent condition would probably be regarded as a mere puff (*Dimmock* v *Hallett* (7)). Equally, the price (£2,000) cannot be regarded as being in any way a statement as to the state or value of the machine.

Given that Percy has a claim for misrepresentation, next one must consider the remedies available to him. It is now one year after the transaction, so it is now probably too late for him to rescind the contract. In *Leaf* v *International Galleries* (8) the Court of Appeal held that lapse of time which barred the right to reject under the Sale of Goods Act was also a bar to rescission for misrepresentation. Percy's only remedy is thus that of damages.

The availability of the remedy of damages depends upon the nature of Victor's misrepresentations. If he was fraudulent then

Percy can recover damages for deceit: *Doyle* v *Olby* (9). However in *Derry* v *Peek* (10) the House of Lords emphasised that the key to fraud was dishonesty and there is no evidence (as opposed to mere suspicion, which is not enough) of dishonesty here.

Next is the question of negligence. Percy can rely on s2(1) of the Misrepresentation Act 1967 which puts the burden of proof on Victor to show that he had reasonable grounds for believing his statements to be true. Failing this, Percy can recover damages under s2(1).

It is submitted that Victor will probably not discharge this burden: he was, after all, a dealer who would have been able to supply a purchaser with accurate information. Under s2(1) Percy's damages will be calculated according to the tortions out of pocket rule: *Andre et Cie* v *Michel Blanc* (11), *Chesnau* v *Interhome* (12) and *Sharneyford Supplies* v *Edge* (13). In money terms he would recover the difference between the price he paid (£2,000) and the true value of the motorcycle. On the facts given, it is not possible to say whether this or the contract measure discussed above would be more favourable to Percy. This would depend on whether a motorcycle as described by Victor would have been worth more or less than £2,000.

For completeness it should be added that if Victor did discharge the evidentiary burden cost on him by s2(1), then Percy would not recover damages for misrepresentation. There is no right to damages where a misrepresentation is neither fraudulent nor negligent, ie innocent only, and the court's power to award damages in lieu of rescission probably does not apply where (as here) the right to rescind is barred in any event.

However, for the reasons already given, one's advice to Percy is that he has good claims for both breach of contract and misrepresentation.

References

1) [1913] AC 30
2) [1964] 1 WLR 623
3) (1848) 1 Ex 855
4) [1977] 1 WLR 1262
5) (1885) 29 Ch D 459
6) (1881) 20 Ch D 1
7) (1866) LR 2 Ch App 21
8) [1950] 2 KB 86
9) (1889) 14 App Cas 337
10) [1969] 2 QB 158

References (continued)

11) [1977] 2 Lloyd's Rep 166
12) (1983) The Times 9 June
13) [1986] Ch 128; [1987] 1 All ER 588

QUESTION 5 (a)

Suggested Solution

It is submitted that the statement in question refers to three quite different situations, namely:

i) where the effect of the mistake is that offer and acceptance do not coincide and there is therefore no true agreement between the parties;

ii) where there is a mistake as to the terms of the offer known to the other party;

iii) where there is a mistake as to identity.

These will be considered in turn.

The classic example of (i) is *Raffles* v *Wichelhaus* (1), where the parties contracted for the sale and purchase of a cargo of cotton on board the ship Peerless from Bombay. There were two ships of this name, each of which had sailed from Bombay carrying cotton. The contracting parties each intended the contract to deal with a different ship. Since it was impossible for the court to say that the subject matter of the contract was either one cargo or the other, the contract was held to be void for mistake.

A less obvious example is *Scriven Bros* v *Hindley* (2) where an auctioneer and bidder intended to deal with different subject-matter. Here the court concluded the contract was void only because the auction catalogue was somewhat ambiguous: but for this the bidder would probably have been stuck with the lot knocked down to him, whether or not he wanted it.

These two cases are variously treated by commentators as being mistake cases or as being offer and acceptance cases. Their classification is probably not so important as the principle that they illustrate, namely that in exceptional cases where the parties are at cross purposes and it is impossible objectively to impute an agreement to them, consent will be negatived and no contract concluded.

Category (ii) derives from the decision of the Court of Queen's Bench in *Smith* v *Hughes* (3) and is best regarded as an exception to the caveat emptor rule and the general principle that one party is under no duty to correct a misapprehension the other may have (unless the former has caused or contributed to it). The rule in *Smith* v *Hughes* is that where one party makes a mistake as to the terms of the contract, and the other knows of that mistake, the contract is void. The rationale for this principle is that not only are the parties not ad idem, but one of them knows they are not ad idem. Thus in *Hartog* v *Colin & Shields* (4), where negotiations for skins had been conducted on the basis of a price per piece, it was held that no contract was concluded where one party purported to accept an offer mistakenly made by the other at a price per pound.

Category (iii), mistake as to the identity, has given rise to a good deal of case law. With some diffidence, it is suggested that the following principles represent the present state of the law.

Where the parties are not physically in each other's presence (eg they are dealing by correspondence), where one party is mistaken as to the identity - not the attributes – of the other and intends instead to deal with some identifiable third party, and the other knows this, then the contract will be void for mistake: *Cundy* v *Lindsay* (5) and *King's Norton Metal* v *Edridge Merritt* (6).

However where the parties are inter praesentes, there is a strong presumption which will rarely, if ever, be rebutted, that the parties intend to deal with the person physically present and identifiable by sight and sound, irrespective of the identity which one or other may assume: *Phillips* v *Brooks* (7) and *Lewis* v *Averay* (8). Nevertheless there is some authority *Lake* v *Simmons* (9) and *Ingram* v *Little* (10) which suggests that in exceptional cases a mistake as to identity inter praesentes can negative consent so as to render a contract void.

References

1) (1864) 2 H & C 906
2) [1913] 3 KB 564
3) (1871) LR 6 QB 597
4) [1939] 3 All ER 566
5) (1878) 3 App Cas 459
6) (1897) 14 TLR 98
7) [1919] 2 KB 243
8) [1872] 1 QB 198
9) [1927] AC 487
10) [1961] 1 QB 31

QUESTION 5 (b)

Suggested Solution

The question here is whether the contract apparently concluded between the computer firm and Professor Albert Higgins is valid or is void for mistake as to identity.

It is a basic principle of the law of contract that an offer can only be accepted by the person to whom it is addressed: *Boulton* v *Jones* (1) and *Hardman* v *Booth* (2). However the law adopts a subjective rather than an objective approach and asks not to whom an offer was intended to be addressed but to whom, objectively speaking, it is to be regarded as having been addressed, *Falck* v *Williams* (3). Thus the fact that the firm intended to address its offer to Professor Andrew Higgins is not conclusive in determining whether or not it was capable of being accepted by Professor Albert. If the latter reasonably believed that the offer was being made to him, then his acceptance of it would be valid: *Upton On Severn UDC* v *Powell* (4).

The significant feature of the facts given is that there had been previous dealings between the firm and Professor Andrew. If the offer made was in some way referable to these dealings (eg by their being mentioned in the letter of offer), then Professor Andrew either knew or should of known that he was not the intended offeree and his purported acceptance would therefore be invalid: *Boulton* v *Jones*. An analogous case is *Cundy* v *Lindsay* (5), in which the House of Lords held that where a party knows that the other party to the contract intends to deal only with some identifiable third party and not with him, any contract will be void for mistake as to identity.

If, on the other hand, there was nothing to put Professor Andrew on notice that he was not the intended offeree, the principle simplified in *Upton* v *Powell* would indicate that a contract was concluded. It is submitted, though, that it would be highly unusual for anyone, no matter how eminent, to receive through the post an offer of a valuable consultancy without there being any prior dealings of communications between the parties. All in all, therefore, whilst the relevant documents would clearly have to be construed with care, it is likely that a court would regard this is a *Boulton* v *Jones* type case and hold that no contract was concluded.

References

1) (1857) 2 H & N 564
2) [1983] 1 H & C 803
3) [1900] AC 176
4) [1942] 1 All ER 220
5) (1878) 3 App Cas 459

QUESTION 6

Suggested Solution

At the outset a preliminary point must be taken in the case of Phil's wife. The contract is between Phil and the tour company. Since she is not a party to it, she cannot sue on it: *Dunlop* v *Selfridge* (1) and *Beswick* v *Beswick* (2). It may be that she would have claims in tort against the company, but a consideration of those is outside the scope of this answer. All that will be said is that as she was not a party to the contract, the company cannot rely on any exclusion clause to defeat her tortious claims: *Scruttons* v *Midlands Silicones* (3).

Now one turns to Phil who was a contracting party. It is submitted that by racing against another driver, the driver of the coach committed (as the company's agent) a breach of contract for which Phil could, in the ordinary course, recover damages from the company. However it is necessary to consider the effect of classes 1 and 2 from the company's terms which may restrict or exclude Phil's rights altogether. In advising Phil one must discuss:

a) whether the clauses were incorporated as terms of the contract;
b) if they were, whether on their true construction they apply to the events which have occurred; and
c) finally, the possible application and effect of the Unfair Contract Terms Act 1977.

First, then, is the issue of incorporation. The facts do not reveal that Phil ever signed a booking form containing either of the clauses (this would be conclusive if he had, *L'Estrange* v *Graucob* (4)), so the question arises whether he was given reasonable notice of them prior to or at the time of the conclusion of the contract, *Parker* v *South Eastern Railway* (5). The clauses are contained on the back of each document given to him. If these documents were delivered contemporaneously with the making of the contract, then the clauses were probably incorporated, *Parker*'s case. If, on the other hand, they were handed over after its conclusion, then this would be too late, *Olley* v *Marlborough Court Hotel* (6) and *Hollingsworth* v *Southern Ferries* (7).

The facts also disclose that the clauses were displayed at the office where Phil booked the holiday. Provided they were displayed with sufficient prominence to draw the attention of the reasonable man to them, then this would suffice to incorporate them: *Watkins* v *Rymill* (8).

The facts given do not enable one to be categorical one way or the other. Suffice to say that there is a real risk that the clauses were incorporated.

Next is the question of construction. Phil has suffered both personal injury and damage to his property. Racing a coach is almost certainly a negligent act, but negligence is explicitly embraced by clause 1. By expressly using the words 'negligent acts', at common law the company has effectively excluded both of Phil's claims: *Alderslade* v *Hendon Laundry* (9) and *Smith* v *South Wales Switchgear* (10). It should also be noted that there is no longer any doctrine of fundamental breach which prevents a clause excluding liability for a breach which goes to the root of the contract: *Photo Production* v *Securicor* (11) and *George Mitchell* v *Finney Lock Seeds* (12).

Thus one comes finally to the 1977 Act. Clearly the Act applies since the company is in the business of providing holidays: s1(3) of the Act.

Phil's first claim is in respect of his broken leg. It has already been observed that this injury was sustained as a result of the company's driver's negligence. Accordingly s2(1) of the Act applies with the consequence that both clauses 1 and 2 are rendered totally ineffective, as that sub-section is an absolute bar to a party excluding or restricting liability for negligence which causes death or personal injury.

Phil's second claim is for damage to his cine-camera. Section 2(2) of the 1977 Act allows the exclusion or restriction of liability for negligence causing damage to (inter alia) property only insofar as the clause satisfies the requirement of reasonableness laid down in s11(1) of the Act. Similarly s3 applies the reasonableness test to clauses which purport to exclude or restrict liability for breach of contract. As Phil was dealing as consumer, and also on the company's standard terms, s3 applies also.

The issue is, therefore, whether the company can rely on clause 1 as a complete defence, or clause 2 as a partial defence to Phil's claim. This involves applying the reasonableness test in s11(1): were these reasonable clauses to include in their contract, judged at the time the contract was concluded, not in the light of subsequent events? As to clause 2, s11(4) raises two specific relevant considerations.

Although the 1977 Act came into force on 1 February 1978, there is still comparatively little law on it. Such cases as there are (eg

Walker v *Boyle* (13) and *Southwestern General Property* v *Marton* (14)) tend to illustrate only that the courts are quite willing to hold wide ranging exclusion clauses to be unreasonable rather than laying down general principles.

The material considerations here are that Phil was a consumer, the risk of liability for injury to passengers would (or should) have been insured against by the company and, in the case of clause 1, all liability is excluded for negligence and, in the case of clause 2, damages recoverable under the heads of liability are limited to what is little more than a nominal sum.

All things considered, it is submitted that the court would be likely to hold that clause 1 was unreasonable, and probably clause 2 as well. Phil could therefore recover damages for the damage to his cine-camera. He could probably also recover damages for distress and disappointment as a result of his holiday being ruined, *Jarvis* v *Swans Tours* (15) and *Jackson* v *Horizon Holidays* (16).

Lastly, is the issue whether Phil as the contracting party could recover damages on behalf of his wife. In *Woodar* v *Wimpey* (17) the House of Lords expressed the view that there was no general rule that where A made a contract with B for the benefit of C, if B broke the contract A could recover damages on behalf of C, disapproving contrary dicta in *Jackson* v *Horizon Holidays*. However certain of their Lordships (Lord Scarman in particular) thought that contracts in a social context, such as holidays, might call for special treatment, and none of them were prepared to say that the decision on the facts in *Jackson* was wrong. Thus based on these observations, it is quite possible that Phil would be able to recover damages on behalf of his wife in respect of her nervous shock, and for disappointment and distress, if she has suffered any.

References

1) [1915] AC 847
2) [1968] AC 58
3) [1962] AC 446
4) [1934] 2 KB 394
5) (1877) 2 CPD 416
6) [1949] 1 KB 532
7) [1977] 2 Lloyd's Rep 70
8) (1883) 10 QBD 178
9) [1945] KB 189
10) [1978] 1 WLR 165
11) [1980] AC 827
12) [1983] 2 AC 803
13) [1982] 1 WLR 495

References (continued)

14) (1982) 263 EG 1090
15) [1973] 1 QB 233
16) [1975] 1 WLR 1468
17) [1980] 1 WLR 227

QUESTION 7

Suggested Solution

One must advise 'The Wild Things' and 'Eatwell' whether their contracts with Lord Blessers were frustrated, and if so what the parties' respective rights and liabilities are.

The doctrine of frustration was introduced into English law by the Court of Queen's Bench in *Taylor* v *Caldwell* (1). In that case, which concerned the hire of a music hall, the court held that it was an implied term of the contract that since the performance of the contract depended upon the continued existence of the music hall, its destruction by fire automatically discharged both parties from their outstanding obligations.

It was for many years considered that the juridical basis of the doctrine of frustration was that stated in *Taylor* v *Caldwell*, namely by implying the appropriate term into a particular contract. Recent decisions of the House of Lords have, however, restated the juridical basis in (it is submitted) a more satisfactory way.

In *Davis Contractors* v *Fareham UDC* (2) Viscount Radcliffe formulated the 'radical change in the obligation theory'. His Lordship formulated the test in the following way: 'Non haec in foedera veri, it was not this that I promised to do.' His Lordship's test has been subsequently adopted and applied in *National Carriers* v *Panalpina* (3) and *The Nema* (4) and is now generally accepted as correctly stating the law of frustration.

This test must therefore be applied to see if the two contracts in question have been frustrated. It should be noted that there is no legal or physical impossibility presenting either contract being performed. The Ministry of Agriculture has appealed to residents on a 'voluntary basis': it has not taken any legal steps to prevent outdoor events taking place.

No doubt it is very public spirited of Lord Blessers to respond to the Ministry's appeal. That, however, does not amount to frustration of either contract. It is not correct to say that either contract is incapable of performance (per Viscount Radcliffe in *Davis* v *Fareham*), both are still well capable of being performed. Cases such as *Tsakiroglou* v *Noblee Thorl* (5), *The Eugenia* (6) and *Davis* v *Fareham* itself indicate that the courts do not readily accede to a plea of frustration. It is submitted a court would not do so here. Alternatively, as it was Lord Blessers who cancelled the contracts, the case could be regarded as one of self-induced frustration: *Maritime National Fish* v *Ocean Trawlers* (7). Accordingly Lord Blessers was not entitled to cancel the contracts and both the group and Eatwell can recover damages from him for breach of contract, either for loss of profit or in respect of expenses thrown away: *CCC Films* v *Impact Quadrant Films* (8).

The alternative set of facts postulates that the bride has been killed a week before the wedding. In these circumstances it is submitted that both contracts would be frustrated. The concert and the meals are part of the intended celebration of the wedding. If the bride is killed, no wedding can take place. The facts as varied are similar to *Krell* v *Henry* (9), where a contract to hire rooms overlooking the route of the coronation procession was held to be frustrated when the coronation was cancelled.

Thus next one must consider the consequences which flow from the contracts being frustrated.

Taking first the group, it is settled law that a frustrating event discharges a contract automatically and immediately: *Hirji Mulji* v *Cheong Yue SS* (10). At common law, the position was that whilst the parties were discharged from any outstanding future obligations, accrued rights and liabilities subsisted and remained enforceable: *Appleby* v *Myers* (11).

The common law principles have been modified, though not entirely replaced, by the Law Reform (Frustrated Contracts) Act 1943, the provisions of which must now be considered in relation to the pop group's concert.

Lord Blessers has paid £1,000 in advance of the due date for performance and prior to the frustrating event. Section 1(2) of the 1943 Act renders this sum recoverable, subject however to the court having a discretion to allow the group to retain all or part of it if it has incurred expense in performance of the contract. In *BP Exploration* v *Hunt (No 2)* (12) Robert Goff J explained this sub-section as giving statutory recognition to the defence of change of position.

The facts disclose that the pop group has spent considerable sums in setting up a stage, so it is possible that the court will allow it to keep all (or certainly part) of the £1,000 paid by Lord Blessers in advance. On the other hand if the group has incurred expenses in excess of this sum, it cannot recover such excess from Lord Blessers under s1(3) of the 1943 Act. Thus the best it can do is to persuade the court to allow it to retain the whole of the £1,000.

The position of Eatwell is even weaker. In this case there have been no advance payments forthcoming or due from but not paid by Lord Blessers, so s1(2) can have no application. Further, again s1(3) as construed in *BP* v *Hunt* does not apply either since Lord Blessers has not received any valuable benefit within the terms of the sub-section.

References

1) (1863) 3 B & S 826
2) [1956] AC 696
3) [1981] AC 675
4) [1982] AC 724
5) [1962] AC 93
6) [1964] 2 QB 226
7) [1935] AC 524
8) [1985] QB 16
9) [1903] 2 KB 740
10) [1926] AC 497
11) (1867) LR 2 CP 651
12) [1979] 1 WLR 783

QUESTION 8 (a)

Suggested Solution

The proposition which falls to be discussed contains, it is submitted, two distinct areas:

i) damages for hurt feelings or disappointment;

ii) damages for injury to reputation.

Until relatively recently, it could be stated with confidence that whilst damages could be awarded for physical inconvenience (eg *Hobbs* v *L & SW Ry* (1)), the decision of the House of Lords in *Addis* v *Gramophone* (2) was conclusive that in contrast damages were not available in respect of mental distress suffered as a result of a breach of contract. A succession of cases starting in 1973 has, however, made substantial inroads into their principle.

First came *Jarvis* v *Swans Tours* (3) and *Jackson* v *Horizon Holidays* (4) in which damages were awarded for distress and disappointment suffered as a result of package holidays falling below the standard promised by the tour operators. In both cases the judgments of the Court of Appeal were on a sufficiently broad basis to warrant the conclusion that henceforth damages could be awarded for distress providing that was something that could reasonably have been contemplated as being a probable consequence of the breach.

These cases were followed and applied in *Cox* v *Philips* (5) in which an employee suffered distress as a result of being wrongfully demoted (*Addis* was distinguished as dealing with wrongful dismissal only), in *Heywood* v *Wellers* (6) where a firm of solicitors failed to start the necessary proceedings to prevent the Plaintiff from being molested by an ex-boyfriend, and in *Perry* v *Sidney Phillips* (7) where a surveyor negligently failed to observe major structural faults in a dwelling house.

It appeared that the courts were assuming a general jurisdiction to award damages for distress until two recent discussions which represent something of a retreat from these advances. In *Shove* v *Downs Surgical* (8) Sheen J applied *Addis* and held that damages were not available for distress in a wrongful dismissal case. Then in *Bliss* v *SE Thames Health Authority* (9) the Court of Appeal overruled *Cox* v *Philips* and held that damages were not generally available for distress in contract, saying that the *Jarvis* line of cases concerned contracts which were either for the provision of pleasure or the alleviation of suffering from which (exceptionally) damages for distress were available. This undoubtedly is a considerable narrowing of the broad statements which are to be found in cases such as *Jarvis* and *Jackson*.

As to injury to reputation, a specific area of law – defamation – provides the appropriate procedures and remedies. Accordingly contract damages are not generally available for injury to reputation consequent upon a breach of contract: *Addis* v *Gramophone*. The only exceptions to this are:

a) where a banker wrongfully dishonours a trader's cheque, *Gibbons* v *Westminster Bank* (10);

b) where an actor suffers loss of publicity and the chance to enhance his reputation, *Clayton* v *Oliver* (11);

c) where an apprentice is wrongfully dismissed before the end of his apprenticeship, *Dunk* v *Waller* (12).

References

1) (1875) LR 10 QB 111
2) [1909] AC 488
3) [1973] QB 233
4) [1975] 1 WLR 1468
5) [1976] 1 WLR 638
6) [1976] QB 446
7) [1982] 1 WLR 1297
8) [1984] ICR 532
9) [1985] IRLR 308
10) [1939] 2 KB 882
11) [1930] AC 209
12) [1970] 2 QB 163

QUESTION 8 (b)

Suggested Solution

In advising A Ltd one must consider whether it can recover damages in respect of i) the cost of repairs; ii) loss of revenue while the complex is closed; and iii) loss of revenue from hosting the world championships.

First, two preliminary points must be made. The contract for the construction of the complex was made between A Ltd and B Ltd. It was the latter who employed the sub-contractors, C Ltd, who used the unsuitable cement. No contractual relationship existed between A Ltd and C Ltd and C Ltd therefore cannot have incurred any liability in contract to A Ltd. since priority of contract did not exist between them. On the other hand it matters not that B Ltd may have acted reasonably in engaging C Ltd and may have believed them to be competent sub-contractors. Liability in contract is strict and if B Ltd have not built or caused the complex to be built in a proper manner, they are in breach of their contract with A Ltd.

Turning now to the items of loss listed (i) to (iii) above, item (i) causes little difficulty. If a building (be it a sports complex or anything else) is incorrectly constructed, it is plain and obvious that the owner is going to incur expense in correcting the fault. Such a head of loss is within the first limb of the rule in *Hadley* v *Baxendale* (1) – loss occurring in the usual course of things – and A Ltd can therefore recover the cost of repair from B Ltd.

Item (ii) is also relatively straightforward. B Ltd must have known that A Ltd wished to have the complex built in order to use it. So long as it is undergoing repairs, it will clearly be out of commission and incapable of being used. The loss of revenue which results is again within the first limb of the rule in *Hadley* v *Baxendale*. Indeed, their head of claim is very similar to the general loss of profits claim which succeeded in *Victoria Laundry* v *Newman Industries* (2), where knowledge of the likely use of the subject matter of the contract to earn revenue was imputed to the contract breaker. Alternatively, adopting the test used by the majority of the Court of Appeal in *Parsons* v *Uttley Ingham* (3), loss of revenue during repair was a serious possibility if the complex was not properly built.

It is the third head of loss, the loss of revenue from possibly holding the World Badminton Championships, which raises most difficulties.

In this regard first it should be noted that although there was no certainty that the complex would play host to the championships, that of itself is no bar to A Ltd recovering damages. Where possible, the courts will put a value on the loss of a chance: *Chaplin* v *Hicks* (4).

The problem regarding this item is that of remoteness. Hosting a world sports championship is something far out of the ordinary for any sports complex. There is a real danger the court would regard this head of loss as being too remote.

Hadley v *Baxendale* is the source of the modern law of remoteness. Clearly this head of loss is not within the first limb of the rule, so is it within the second limb viz something the parties could have contemplated as being the probable result of the breach? As explained in *Victoria Laundry* (a part of the case approved by the House of Lords in *The Heron II* (5), remoteness depends on knowledge and the second limb of the rule is concerned with actual knowledge of special circumstances which make additional loss (over and above loss arising in the ordinary course of things) likely.

It is submitted that the possibility of A Ltd hosting the world championships was so unlikely that unless B Ltd had actual knowledge of this possibility, the lost revenue is irrecoverable (by analogy with the lucrative dyeing contracts in *Victoria Laundry*). Alternatively, to apply the test of Orr and Searman LJJ in *Parsons*, it was not something both parties could have contemplated at the time the contract was concluded as being a serious possibility in the event that B Ltd was in breach. This third head of loss is, therefore, irrecoverable.

References

1) (1854) 9 Ex 34
2) [1949] 2 KB 528
3) [1978] QB 791
4) [1911] 2 KB 786
5) [1969] 1 AC 530

QUESTION 9

Suggested Solution

In *Petrofina Ltd* v *Martin* (1) Diplock LJ (as he then was) defined a contract in restraint of trade as being one in which a party (the covenantor) agrees with the other (the covenantee) to restrict his liberty in future to trade with others in such manner as he chooses. From this broad definition, it can be seen that the doctrine of restraint of trade can operate in an infinite variety of situations. This answer will consider some of the more notable ones and the application principles in each case.

However, before looking at particular examples of the application of the doctrine, some general principles which apply in all cases can be briefly stated.

In *Nordenfelt* v *Maxim Nordenfelt* (2), the starting point for any analysis of the modern law of restraint of trade, the House of Lords held that all contracts in restraint of trades are prima facie unenforceable, that there is no difference between a partial and a total restraint and that it is a question of law whether in any given case the circumstances justify the restraint which is sought to be imposed, judged at the time the contract was concluded. Further, their Lordships held that for a restraint to be justified it had to be both reasonable as between the parties (as to which the burden of proof is on the covenantee) and also reasonable in the interests of the public (where the burden of proof is on the covenantor).

To these principles may be added certain propositions derived from a late House of Lords decision, *Esso Petroleum* v *Harper's Garage* (3), where their Lordships stressed that the categories of contracts to which the doctrine applies are not closed and that it can apply as well to the use of land as to the activities of an individual.

Now some examples of contracts in restraint of trade can be considered.

The most common example is that of a covenant contained in a contract of employment whereby an employer seeks to restrict his employee's activities after termination of the employment.

Employer – employee covenants are of broadly three types:

i) Covenants restraining the use of confidential information. Even in the absence of an express obligation, an employee will usually be under an implied duty not to disclose or make use of confidential information: *Faccenda Chicken* v *Fowler* (4). However an express covenant has the advantage of drawing the employee's attention to this duty, and providing the information can properly be regarded as confidential and being the property of the employer (*Printers & Finishers* v *Holloway* (5)), the covenant will usually be enforced.

ii) Non-solicitation covenants. These too are normally regarded as unobjectionable by the courts providing (a) the employee has had contact with and acquired influences over customers and (b) it is limited to soliciting persons who were customers of the employer whilst the employee worked for him: *Konski* v *Peet* (6). Although such covenants are often defined as to area and direction, consideration of time and space are not usually considered crucial: *Plowman* v *Ash* (7).

iii) Covenants against doing business. These are the most drastic and wide ranging types of covenant because they effectively prevent the employee from earning his living in the same field as his employer. Because of this sterilising effect, the courts scrutinise them with particular care. Matters to which the courts especially have regard are the areas to which the covenant extends, its duration, the activity restrained and the seniority or otherwise of the position held by the employee. Essentially the courts have to embark on a balancing exercise, considering on the one hand the necessity of preventing the employer from obtaining an unfair advantage over his employee and on the other the desirability of allowing every man to earn his living as he chooses.

Consequently each case turns on is particular facts and reported decisions can only be a guide to future cases. Thus in *Mason* v *Provident Clothing* (8) an area within 25 miles of Islington was regarded as being too wide, whereas in *Forster* v *Suggett* (9) a nationwide and in *Nordenfelt* a worldwide restraint was upheld. Similarly in *Fitch* v *Dewes* (10) a lifelong restraint was considered reasonable, yet in *M & S Drapers* v *Reynolds* (11) a five year restraint was unenforceable. In each of these cases the court struck the balance between the parties' and the public interest in a different way.

Finally on employer-employee covenants, it should be noted that in certain cases the doctrine of severance applied such that it may be possible to delete the offending part and leave behind a reasonable and enforceable covenant: *Goldsoll* v *Goldman* (12). However severance must not remove the bulk of the contractual consideration supplied by one party, *Alec Lobb* v *Total Oil* (13), nor can the court rewrite the covenant, *Attwood* v *Lamont* (14).

Not dissimilar principles to those discussed above apply to covenants in contracts for the sale of a business (*Vancouver Malt* v *Vancouver Breweries* (15)) or in partnership agreements (*Bridge* v *Deacons* (16)). Here, though, the courts take a less strict line, since generally in such cases the parties will have been in more equal bargaining positions than in employer-employee cases.

A relatively recent example of a contract to which the doctrine applies is that of solus petrol agreements. A succession of cases from the mid-1960s show that the doctrine may apply to an exclusive dealing agreement between a petrol station and an oil company. The courts have enumerated the following distinction. The doctrine will apply to a solus tie whereby a person in occupation of land restricts his freedom to trade; it will not apply where the solus tie is contained in a conveyance or lease whereby a person acquires the right to occupy land, albeit subject to that restriction: *Esso* v *Harpers*.

Although the validity of this distinction has been questioned by some commentators, it has been adopted and applied in later cases, eg *Cleveland* v *Dartstone* (17) and *Texaco* v *Mulberry Filling Station* (18). The courts have, however, been astute to prevent oil companies taking advantage of this distinction by devising elaborate schematic transactions such as a lease and lease-back (*Amoco* v *Rocca Bros* (19)) or a lease and lease-back to a company specifically incorporated for this purpose (*Alec Lobb*).

Lastly, simply to show the wide variety of situations to which the doctrine has been applied one might refer to *Eastham* v *Newcastle United FC* (20). (Football Association's player transfer system held unenforceable), *Greig* v *Insole* (21) (ban on cricketers who joined Mr Packer's 'circus' likewise) and *Schroeder Music Publishing* v *Macaulay* (22) (grossly disadvantageous contract between a music publisher and a songwriter struck down). Thus although the doctrine applies to certain commonly encountered types of contract, it can apply to unusual and one-off instances as well.

References

1) [1966] Ch 146
2) [1894] AC 535
3) [1968] AC 269
4) [1986] 1 All ER 617
5) [1965] 1 WLR 1

References (continued)

6) [1915] 1 Ch 530
7) [1964] 1 WLR 568
8) [1913] AC 724
9) (1918) 35 TLR 87
10) [1921] 2 AC 158
11) [1957] 1 WLR 9
12) [1915] 1 Ch 292
13) [1985] 1 All ER 303
14) [1920] 3 KB 571
15) [1934] AC 181
16) [1984] AC 705
17) [1969] 1 WLR 116
18) [1972] 1 WLR 814
19) [1975] AC 561
20) [1964] Ch 413
21) [1978] 1 WLR 302
22) [1974] 1 WLR 1308

UNIVERSITY OF LONDON
INTERMEDIATE EXAMINATION IN LAWS 1988
for External Students

ELEMENTS OF THE LAW OF CONTRACT

Wednesday, 15 June: 10.00 am to 1.00 pm

Answer *FOUR* of the following SEVEN questions.

[Candidates are not required to display any knowledge of the Consumer Credit Act 1974 or the Consumer Protection Act 1987.]

1 Alban manufactures office equipment. Earlier this year he developed a revolutionary stapler. On May 18 he telexed Bruno and David, both wholesalers whom he had dealt with previously, asking each of them whether he would be interested in becoming sole distributor of the staplers. On May 20 Bruno and David each telexed Alban independently stating that he was interested in becoming sole distributor for the stapler and would like further information.

On May 22 Alban telexed Bruno: 'I offer you the post of sole distributor of the stapler at a basic 10% commission. If I hear nothing from you by May 31, I will assume that this is acceptable to you.'

Bruno immediately posted a first class letter to Alban in which he accepted Alban's offer. The letter did not arrive until June 2.

Meanwhile on May 31 David, having heard nothing from Alban since the telex of May 18, posted a letter to Alban in which David offered to become Alban's sole distributor for a 5% commission.

Alban received David's letter on June 1. Alban immediately telephoned Bruno and told him that the post of sole distributor was no longer available. Bruno insists that there is a binding contract to appoint him.

Advise Alban who wishes to appoint David as sole distributor.

2 'It is not hardship or inconvenience or material loss itself which calls the principle of frustration into play. There must be as well

such a change in the significance of the obligation that the thing undertaken would, if performed, be a different thing then that contracted for.'

Explain and comment.

3 Urban, a window cleaner, hired a ladder from Vitus Equipment Hire Ltd to use while painting the outside of his house. He paid a deposit of £20 and was given a receipt on which was stated: 'Conditions of hire. Vitus accepts no responsibility for any loss or damage suffered as a result of the use of the equipment. Hirers use the equipment at their own risk'. Because of a defective rung on the ladder, Urban fell of it and landed on an expensive radio that he was listening to while he worked. Urban suffered a broken leg and the radio was badly damaged.

Advise Urban. How would your answer differ if he had hired the ladder for use in cleaning windows and had been doing that when the accident happened?

4 'If the parties to a contract are labouring under a common mistake of fact when the contract is made the contract is valid but equity may set it aside.'

Explain and comment.

5 Fab Five Freddy is a disc jockey. He agreed to work last Wednesday night at the Red Lion Club. The Club agreed to provide Freddy with all the necessary equipment for his show including a selection of fifty records. The Club also agreed to pay Freddy £60 for his performance on Wednesday and to pay Bill, Freddy's mate, £20 for Bill's work in setting up the equipment before Freddy went on stage and taking it down afterwards. Bill was not a party to the contract between the Club and Freddy.

On Wednesday Bill arrived at the Red Lion early and set up the equipment for Freddy. However when Freddy arrived he found that there was only a selection of thirty records available. He thereupon informed Richard, the manager of the Red Lion, that he refused to perform and left.

Richard was furious. He told Bill to leave the equipment set up and began telephoning around to find another disc jockey for the evening. He eventually contacted a disc jockey called Super Sally who agreed to perform at the Red Lion that evening for £100. Richard agreed to pay her this fee but when she arrived at the Club Richard found that Bill had taken down the disc jockey equipment and gone home. Richard was forced to pay two local boys £35 each to set up the equipment for Sally. Sally then performed that evening and was very successful.

Freddy and Bill are demanding their fees of £60 and £20 from the Red Lion Club. Richard has refused to pay them and is threatening legal action by the Red Lion Club (which is a limited company) against Freddy for breach of contract.

Discuss.

6 Simon is seventeen. He lives in an isolated village and has recently been offered a job as a sales assistant in the nearest town, which is 15 miles from the village. As there is no bus service, he agreed to buy a used car from Finan Motors for £500. Two days later he discovered that he would be able to get a lift to work from a friend. He then told Finan Motors that he no longer needed the car and would not collect it or pay for it.

Simon also bought a personal stereo a set of golf clubs from General Trading plc. He has paid for the stereo but not the clubs. Because of a fault the stereo has damaged an irreplaceable tape of great sentimental value.

Consider Simon's rights and liabilities in respect of the car, the stereo and the golf clubs.

7 Giles engaged Illtyd, a landscape gardener, to construct a patio and fish pond in his garden for a fixed price of £3,000. The contract provided that the work was to be completed by April 30, 1988 and that payment was to be made in stages as the work proceeded.

In order to pay Illtyd, Giles borrowed £3,000 from Peter, agreeing to repay this sum, together with interest of £720, in twenty four equal monthly instalments.

In March, while Illtyd was excavating the ground for the pond, he uncovered an ancient cannon which he could only remove by using special lifting equipment and he informed Giles that he could only continue with the work if Giles agreed to pay an additional £500. Giles objected but agreed to pay.

Soon after this Giles was made redundant. Peter then agreed that Giles need pay only the interest of the loan until he found a new job. Although Giles is still out of work he recently received a letter from Peter demanding immediate payment of the outstanding arrears of capital and the immediate resumption of payments of instalments at the agreed rate. Illtyd is also pressing for payment of the additional £500.

Advise Giles.

QUESTION 1

Suggested Solution

The question here is whether there is a concluded contract between Alban and Bruno or whether Alban is free to conclude a contract with David.

To answer this question it is necessary to conduct the traditional analysis of offer and acceptance. Lord Denning MR has suggested in *Butler Machine Tool Co Ltd* v *Ex-cell-o Corporation (England) Ltd* (1) and in *Gibson* v *The Manchester City Council* (2) that in many cases the traditional analysis of offer acceptance and so forth is out of date. In the latter case, however, in the House of Lords, Lord Diplock stated that although there may be certain types of contract which do not fit into the normal analysis of a contract as being constituted by offer and acceptance these were exceptional and a contract made by an exchange of correspondence between the parties was not one of these. It is submitted, therefore, that the traditional approach is required in this case.

It is clear that the initial telex from Alban and the replies of Bruno and David to that telex communication are merely preliminary negotiations and can in no way be considered contractual offers or acceptances. This does not require further elaboration.

Alban's telex to Bruno of 22 May is, it is submitted, an offer. Treitel defines an offer as 'an expression of willingness to contract on certain terms made with the intention that it shall become binding as soon as it is accepted by the person to whom it is addressed' (3). Clearly Alban's telex of 22 May accords with this definition. The question is: has Bruno accepted the offer?

An acceptance is a final and unequivocal assent to the terms of an offer. There appears to have been an *act* of acceptance on Bruno's part. When he posts the letter to Alban he clearly indicates by his conduct that he wishes to accept Alban's offer. The question is: has there been communication of the acceptance?

Alban appears to be saying that silence shall be deemed to be acceptance of his offer. *Felthouse* v *Bindley* (4) is authority for the proposition that silence cannot be imposed on the offeree. But this rule has been established for the protection of the offeree who should not be put to the trouble or possible expense of rejecting an offer. But whilst silence cannot be imposed on the offeree, this is not an argument for protecting an offeror who waives communication of acceptance. It could be argued here that Bruno, by his conduct, had accepted the offer and, alternatively, that Alban by virtue of the terms of the offer and Bruno's reliance on the offer was estopped from denying that his offer had been accepted. If this estoppel does operate in Bruno's favour it could, therefore, be argued that by merely posting the letter Bruno has accepted David's offer and that a contract has therefore been concluded between them. It could be objected that estoppel does not create a cause of action but Chitty does not regard this as a serious objection (5).

If the estoppel argument does not hold up, it remains to consider whether the posting of the letter by Bruno constitutes a communication of the acceptance. This requires discussion of the rule relating to acceptances through the post. The rule established in *Adams* v *Lindsell* (6) is that where there has been communication through the post the acceptance is complete as soon as the letter has been posted. If the postal rule applies the contract is concluded even though the letter of acceptance never reaches the offeror: *Household Fire Insurance Co Ltd* v *Grant* (7). The postal rule only applies if it was, in the circumstances, reasonable to use the post: *Henthorn* v *Fraser* (8). There is authority for the view that it would not normally be reasonable to attempt to accept a telegraphic offer by posting a letter; *Quenerduaine* v *Cole* (9). It might therefore be suggested that it would be equally unreasonable to reply to a telex by posting a letter. It is submitted however that this argument cannot be sustained in view of the fact that Alban waived communication of acceptance. Moreover Alban appears to have given Bruno nine days in which to consider whether or not he wishes to reject the offer.

It is trite law that an offer can be revoked at any time before acceptance. But the revocation must be communicated before communication of the acceptance: *Byrne & Co* v *Leon van Tienhoven* (10). Alban purports to revoke the offer on 1 June. However it has been submitted that as Alban has waived communication of acceptance and as Bruno has relied on that waiver, Alban is estopped from denying the validity of Bruno's acceptance. Moreover if the postal rule applied acceptance is deemed to be communicated when the letter is posted, not when it is received. The postal rule can be excluded by the terms of the offer: *Holwell Securities Ltd* v *Hughes* (11). In contrast to that case, however, so far from requiring actual communication of the acceptance, Alban has waived such communication.

Accordingly it is submitted that Alban has a binding contract with Bruno and is, consequently, not free to be able to make an offer to David.

References

1) [1979] 1 WLR 401
2) [1979] 1 WLR 294
3) *Law of Contract* (7th ed) p7
4) (1862) 11 CB (NS) 869
5) *Chitty on Contracts,* para 81
6) (1818) 1 B & Ald 681
7) (1879) 4 Ex D 216
8) [1892] 2 Ch 27
9) (1883) 32 WR 185
10) (1880) 5 CPD 344
11) [1974] 1 WLR 155

QUESTION 2

Suggested Solution

This question requires a discussion of the test that the courts will employ to determine whether or not a contract is frustrated. Prior to 1863, contractual obligations were regarded as absolute. In *Paradine* v *Jane* (1) a tenant was held liable to pay the rental notwithstanding that he had been expelled from the premises by enemy invasion. In English law the concept of frustration was first recognised in the case of *Taylor* v *Caldwell* (2) where the defendants had agreed to let the plaintiffs have the use of a music hall. After the conclusion of the agreement and before the performance of the contract the hall was destroyed by fire. Blackburn J held that because the music hall had ceased to exist without fault of either party both parties were discharged from their further obligations.

The basis of the decision in *Taylor* v *Caldwell* was the implied term theory; the parties had contracted on the basis of the continued existence of the music hall.

The implied term theory was adopted in later cases, see, for example *Blackburn Bobbin Co Ltd* v *TW Allen & Sons Ltd* (3). Here the defendants had agreed to sell to the plaintiffs a certain quantity of Finland birch timber. It was the custom of the defendants to import that timber direct from Finland and this became impossible because of the outbreak of war. This practice was, however, unknown to the plaintiffs and it was held by the Court of Appeal that there was nothing to show that the plaintiffs contemplated that the sellers were adopting this practice. Accordingly the contract was not frustrated.

The implied term theory has now largely been discarded in favour of the 'radical change in obligations' test. This test was first enunciated by Lord Radcliff in *Davis Contractors Ltd* v *Fareham Urban District Council* (4) where his Lordship said that 'frustration occurs whenever the law recognises that without default of either party a contractual obligation has become incapable of being performed because the circumstances in which performance is called for would render it a thing radically different from that which was undertaken by the contract. Non haec in foedera veni. It was not this that I promised to do.'

This test has been approved by two further decisions of the House of Lords: *National Carriers Ltd* v *Panalpina (Northern) Ltd* (5) and *The Nema* (6).

It has been repeatedly emphasised that a contract will not be frustrated merely because it becomes more difficult or expensive to perform. In *Davis* the contractors had entered into a contract with the council to build 78 houses for the sum of £92,425 within a period of eight months. Owing to unexpected circumstances and without the fault of either party there was a serious shortage of skilled labour and of building materials and the work took 22 months to complete, with the result that the contractors unavoidably incurred considerable additional expense. The delay and consequent further expense was not, however, sufficient to frustrate the contract. In *The Eugenia* (7) Lord Denning MR said 'the fact that it has become more onerous or more expensive for one party than he thought is not sufficient to bring about a frustration. It must be more than merely more onerous or more expensive. It must be positively unjust to hold the parties bound.' Lord Denning also observed that the implied term theory had been discarded by nearly everyone for the simple reason that it did not represent the truth. In that case if the parties had contemplated the occurrence of the event they would not have said 'it is all over between us'. They would have differed about what was to happen, so that there was no room for an implied term.

There will be a frustrating event if the subject matter of the contract is physically destroyed as in *Taylor* v *Caldwell* (above) or if there is a supervening legal impossibility: *Metropolitan Water Board* v *Dick, Kerr & Co Ltd* (8); *Denny, Mott & Dickson Ltd* v *James B Fraser & Co Ltd* (9).

Frustration is not, however, confined to physical or legal impossibility. The contract will also be frustrated if performance has become fundamentally different in a commercial sense: *Tsakiroglou & Co Ltd* v *Noblee Thorl* (10). In *Jackson* v *Union Marine Insurance Co Ltd* (11) a ship, the subject matter of the contract, ran aground and the consequent repairs took over six months to complete. It was held that the delay was so long as to put an end in a commercial sense to the commercial speculation entered upon by the parties. In *Krell* v *Henry* (12) the defendant had hired a room to witness the coronation procession of King Edward VII. Owing to the King's illness the coronation was postponed. The contract was held to be frustrated on the grounds that the state of things which the parties contemplated was no longer in existence. A contrasting case, also arising out of the postponed coronation of King Edward VII, was that of *Herne Bay Steam Boat*

Company v *Hutton* (13). In that case the defendant hired a board in order to witness a royal naval revue. Owing to the postponement of the coronation the review was cancelled. However the fleet was still there and it was held that the doctrine of frustration did not apply in these circumstances.

Finally it must be noted that the event in question must have arisen without the fault of either party. The doctrine cannot be relied on if the frustration is self induced: *Maritime National Fish Ltd* v *Ocean Trawlers Ltd* (14): *Paal Wilson* v *Blumenthal* (15).

References

1) (1647) Aleyn 26
2) (1863) 3 B & S 826
3) [1918] 2 KB 467
4) [1956] AC 696
5) [1981] AC 675
6) [1981] 3 WLR 292
7) [1964] 2 QB 226
8) [1918] AC 119
9) [1944] AC 265
10) [1962] AC 93
11) (1874) LR 10 CP 125
12) [1903] 2 KB 740
13) [1903] 2 KB 683
14) [1935] AC 524
15) [1983] AC 854

QUESTION 3

Suggested Solution

This question involves an examination of the effect of the 'Conditions of hire' in the receipt handed to Urban which purports to exclude liability for loss or damage resulting from the use of the ladder. In order to decide on the validity of this exclusion clause it is necessary to pursue three stages of investigation: (i) whether the clause has been incorporated in to the contract; (ii) whether the clause, as a matter of construction, covers the breach of contract that has occurred; and (iii) if the answer to both these questions is in the affirmative, whether the clause will be rendered ineffective by the provisions of the Unfair Contract Terms Act 1977.

Incorporation

Where, as in the present case, the relevant document has not been signed by the party concerned, it has to be determined whether or not the party sought to be bound by the exclusion clause has been given reasonable notice of it: *Parker* v *South Eastern Railway* (1). To answer this, one has to decide if the receipt can be considered to be a contractual document and if notice of it was given before the contract was concluded. In *Chapelton* v *Barry Urban District Council* (2) a receipt furnished on the hire of a deck chair was held not to be a contractual document. But cloak room tickets and railway tickets have been held to have contractual effect: *Alexander* v *Railway Executive* (3); *Thompson* v *London, Midland and Scottish Railway* (4). Much depends on the nature of the particular transaction. Whilst it is not possible to give a categorical answer, it is submitted that, given the type and cost of the equipment in this problem, the receipt could be expected to have contractual effect, provided that it was given to Urban before the conclusion of the contract. An exclusion clause will not be deemed to be incorporated if notice of it is given after the contract has been concluded: *Olley* v *Marlborough Court Hotel* (5); *Thornton* v *Shoe Lane Parking Ltd* (6). It is not clear from the facts that have been given when the contract between Urban and the Company was concluded, but it is assumed for the sake of argument that the receipt was given prior to or simultaneously with the conclusion of the contract.

If the clause was incorporated into the contract it is necessary to proceed to the next stage of investigation.

Construction of the exclusion clause

Two aspects have to be considered; firstly whether the defect in the ladder was caused by the negligence of the Company, and secondly what other breach of contract the Company has committed.

There is clear authority for the proposition that where a party can be held liable on some ground other than negligence the clause will be construed as excluding liability on that ground and not for negligence: *Alderslade* v *Hendon Laundry* (7); *Gillespie Brothers* v *Roy Bowles Transport* (8); *Hollier* v *Rambler Motors* (9). As there is another ground on which the Company can be held liable it is submitted that the contra proferentum rule would be applied here and that the clause would not cover liability for negligence. Even if it did, as far as Urban's personal injuries are concerned, the clause would be ineffective by virtue of s2(1) Unfair Contract Terms Act. However, as there is no indication either way as to negligence on the part of the Company, this aspect cannot be pursued further.

The Company has hired the ladder to Urban in the course of a business. Under s9(2) Supply of Goods and Services Act 1982 there is an implied condition that the ladder is of merchantable quality. The Company appears clearly to be in breach of this implied term. They may also be in breach of the condition that the ladder is fit for a particular purpose which is implied by s9(5) of that Act, but this does not take the matter any further.

The clause appears wide enough to cover this breach. It is now settled law that there is no breach of contract so 'fundamental' that liability for its breach cannot be excluded as a matter of law; the question is always one of construction. The authority for this is three decisions of the House of Lords: *Suisse Atlantique Societe D'Armament Maritime* v *Rotterdamsche Kolen Centrale* (10); *Photo Production Ltd* v *Securicor Transport Ltd* (11); *George Mitchell (Chesterhall) Ltd* v *Finney Lock Seeds Ltd* (12). In *Suisse Atlantique* it was observed that as a rule of construction an exclusion clause should not, in the absence of clear words, be applied to breaches which tend to defeat the main purpose of the contract. But the clause here has been drafted in very wide terms and it would be difficult to argue that it could not be applied to the breach.

The Unfair Contract Terms Act

The Act does apply here as the liability which the Company seeks to exclude is a business liability – s1(3).

As has already been noted, if the defect in the ladder arose from the negligence of the Company, the exclusion of liability in respect of Urban's broken leg would be totally ineffective. Liability for negligence in respect of the damage to Urban's radio could only be excluded in so far as the clause satisfies the requirement of reasonableness – s2(2). This requirement is discussed below.

Liability for negligence is doubtful, but the Company is clearly in breach of the implied conditions referred to above. It remains to consider the effect of the Act in this regard.

By virtue of s7(2), liability in respect of the ladder's quality or fitness for any particular purpose cannot be excluded as against a person dealing as a consumer. Under s12(1) a party deals as a consumer if he neither makes the contract in the course of a business nor holds himself out as doing so, and the other party does make the contract in the course of a business. It seems clear that, if Urban hired the ladder to use while painting his house, he was dealing as a consumer, and that, therefore, the Company's attempt to exclude liability for its breach of contract would be rendered ineffective under s7(2). The Company would consequently be liable to Urban for the damages he has suffered.

If Urban had hired the ladder for use in cleaning windows, and had been doing that when the accident happened, the question arises as to whether he would then be regarded as dealing as a consumer. Prima facie it would appear that he would then be deemed to have made the contract in the course of a business. This, however, it not beyond doubt in view of the decision in *R & B Customs Brokers Co Ltd* v *United Dominions Trust Ltd* (13), where the Court of Appeal held that where a transaction was only incidental to a business activity, a degree of regularity was required before the transaction could be said to be an integral part of the business and so carried on in the course of that business. If the hiring of the ladder is considered merely incidental to Urban's business, and there is insufficient regularity in his making such hirings, then he may still be regarded as dealing as a consumer, with the consequences that have been mentioned.

However it is arguable that the hiring of a ladder by a window cleaner is an integral and not an incidental part of his business, and that Urban would not be regarded as dealing as a consumer. In that event the relevant section of the Act is s7(3), which provides that the Company's liability can be excluded only in so far as the clause satisfies the requirement of reasonableness.

The requirement of reasonableness laid down in s11(1) is that the exclusion clause shall have been fair and reasonable 'having regard to the circumstances which were, or ought reasonably to have been, known to or in the contemplation of the parties when the contract was made.' Reasonableness has therefore to be judged by reference to the time of contracting. Under s11(5) the burden of proving that the clause is reasonable is on the Company. For the purposes of s7(3), inter alia, s11(2) requires that regard shall be had to the matters specified in Schedule 2 to the Act, in order to determine the reasonableness or otherwise of the clause. The matters specified in Schedule 2 which are relevant to this problem are: (a) the relative strength of the bargaining positions of the parties; (b) whether Urban received an inducement to agree to the clause, or in accepting it had an opportunity to enter into a similar contract with someone else, but without having to accept a similar clause; and (c) whether Urban knew or ought reasonably to have known of the existence and extent of the term. In the *George Mitchell* case (above) it was indicated that the courts would also take into account the resources of the parties concerned, and the availability of insurance to the party seeking to rely on the clause. It is submitted that little guidance can be obtained from other decisions on very different facts as to whether the present clause meets the requirement of reasonableness. It is at least arguable that, given the wide nature of the clause and the probable inequality of relative bargaining strength, the clause would not be regarded as meeting the requirement. In that event the clause would be ineffective and the Company would be liable to Urban for the damages he has suffered, even if he is not considered to be dealing as a consumer.

References

1) (1977) 2 CPD 416
2) [1940] 1 KB 532
3) [1951] 2 KB 882
4) [1930] 1 KB 41
5) [1949] 1 KB 532
6) [1971] 2 QB 163
7) [1945] KB 189
8) [1973] QB 400
9) [1972] 2 QB 71
10) [1967] 1 AC 361
11) [1980] AC 827
12) [1983] 2 AC 803
13) [1988] 1 All ER 847

QUESTION 4

Suggested Solution

The assumption behind the quotation in this question is that the landmark decision of the House of Lords in *Bell* v *Lever Brothers Ltd* (1) has virtually eliminated the possibility of common mistake rendering the contract void at common law. It is submitted that the statement in the quotation is misleading, and in order to support this submission it will be convenient to examine common mistake under four headings.

i) Mistake as to the existence of the subject matter.

ii) Mistake as to title.

iii) Mistake based on a false and fundamental assumption.

iv) Mistake as to quality.

i) *Mistake as to the existence of the subject matter*

A contract will be void if the subject matter of the contract never existed or had ceased to exist at the time the contract was concluded. With regard to sale of goods, s6 Sale of Goods Act 1979 provides:

> 'Where there is a contract for the sale of specific goods, and the goods without the knowledge of the seller have perished at the time when the contract is made, the contract is void.'

At common law *Couturier* v *Hastie* (2) is authority for the view that mistake as to the existence of the subject matter makes the contract void. Whilst the concept of the mistake was not the basis of the judgment in that case, indeed the word 'mistake' was not used in the judgments, there are clear indications in the decisions that the contract would be void for mistake. In his speech in the House of Lords, Lord Cranworth LC said that the whole question turned upon the construction of the contract which was entered into between the parties. The Lord Chancellor said that the contract plainly imported that there was something which was to be sold at the time of the contract, and something to be purchased. As no such thing existed, the Lord Chancellor clearly implied that the contract was void.

In *McRae* v *Commonwealth Disposals Commission* (3) the High Court of Australia was able to distinguish the facts before it from *Couturier* v *Hastie*. There it was held that, as a matter of construction of the contract, there was an implied undertaking that the tanker existed. Whether or not *McRae* can be reconciled with *Couturier* is still a matter for argument. An explanation of the decision in *McCrae* is given by Steyn J in *Associated Japanese Bank* v *Credit du Nord* (4) where His Lordship suggested that a party should not be able to rely on a common mistake where he had no reasonable grounds for the belief.

ii) *Mistake as to title*
In *Cooper* v *Phibbs* (5), A agreed to take a lease of a fishery from B though, contrary to the belief of both parties at the time, A was tenant for life of the fishery and B apparently had no title at all. This mistake rendered the contract void. Lord Atkin in *Bell* thought that mistake as to title corresponded to mistake as to the existence of the subject matter.

iii) *False and fundamental assumption*
There are circumstances where the parties share a false and fundamental assumption going to the route of the contract, and because of that mistake, the contract will be void. In *Griffith* v *Brymer* (6) the parties had entered into an agreement for the hire of a room to view the coronation procession of King Edward VII. However, the decision to operate on the King, which caused the cancellation of the procession, had been taken prior to the conclusion of the contract. It was held that the agreement was made on a missupposition of facts which went to the whole root of the matter the contract. (It is perhaps doubtful whether this decision can stand with *Bell* v *Lever Brothers Ltd.*) In *Scott* v *Coulson* (7) a contract for the assignment of a policy of life insurance concluded on the shared mistaken belief that the assured was still alive was held to be void for mistake. In *Galloway* v *Galloway* (8) a separation deed entered into by the parties on the mistaken assumption they had a valid marriage was also held to be void. The above three cases were heard before *Bell*. However in *Sheik Brothers Ltd* v *Ochsner* (9) a contract was held to be void for mistake because of an initial commercial impossibility. The case was decided under s20 Indian Contract Act 1872 but the Privy Council expressly applied the principles laid down in *Bell*.

iv) *Mistake as to quality*
It does appear that mistake as to quality will rarely make the contract void at common law: see the authorities prior to *Bell* of *Kennedy* v *Panama Royal Mail Co* (10) and *Smith* v *Hughes* (11). The decision in *Bell* turned on the question of mistake as to

quality, and it is suggested in Cheshire, Fifoot and Furmston's *Law of Contract* (12) that if the mistake in that case did not make the contract void, it would be difficult to envisage circumstances in which a contract would ever be void for mistake as to quality. In *Associated Japanese Bank* Steyn J suggested that this conclusion did not do justice to the speeches in *Bell.* Lord Atkin had held in *Bell* that:

> '... a mistake will not affect assent unless it is the mistake of both parties and is as to the existence of some quality which makes the thing without the quality essentially different from the thing it was believed to be.'

Since the decision in *Bell* it has proved difficult for the courts to find a contract void for mistake as to quality: *Leaf* v *International Galleries* (13); *Harrison & Jones* v *Bunten and Lancaster* (14). In *Nicholson & Venn* v *Smith-Marriot* (15) and in *Peco Arts Inc* v *Hazlitt Galleries Ltd* (16) the court would have been prepared to find the contracts in those cases void for mistake as to quality, but in neither case did the decision turn on that point.

In *Associated Japanese Bank* Steyn J would also have been prepared to find the contract void for mistake as to quality, but again His Lordship decided the matter on other grounds. In the course of his judgment Steyn J suggested a number of guiding principles.

a) The first imperative was that the law ought to uphold rather than destroy apparent contracts.

b) The common law rules as to a mistake regarding the quality of the subject matter, like the common law rules regarding commercial frustration, are designed to cope with the impact of unexpected and wholly exceptional circumstances on apparent contracts.

c) Such a mistake must be substantially shared by both parties, and must relate to facts as they existed at the time the contract was made.

d) As established by *Bell* v *Lever Brothers Ltd* the mistake must render the subject matter of the contract essentially and radically different from the subject matter which the parties believed to exist.

e) A party cannot be allowed to rely on a common mistake where the mistake consists of a belief which is entertained by him without any reasonable grounds for such a belief. With regard to the latter point Steyn J referred to *McRae* v *Commonwealth Disposals Commission.*

Whilst there are circumstances in which a contract will be held to be void at common law for mistake, such circumstances appear to be limited and somewhat uncertain. Even where the contract is not void at common law, however, equity may be able to provide relief. In *Solle* v *Butcher* (17) Lord Denning MR said that:

> 'A contract is also liable in equity to be set aside if the parties were under a common misapprehension either as to the facts or as to their relative and respective rights, provided that the misapprehension was fundamental and that the party seeking to set it aside was not himself at fault.'

The correctness of the decision in *Solle* v *Butcher* has been doubted, see for example *Amalgamated Investment & Property Co Ltd* v *John Walker and Sons Ltd* (18). However, the equitable jurisdiction has become firmly established. The principles of *Solle* v *Butcher* have been considered and applied in the later cases of *Grist* v *Bailey* (19), *Magee* v *Pennine Insurance Co Ltd* (20) and *Laurence* v *Lexcourt Holdings Ltd* (21). According to that jurisdiction a contract may be voidable for common mistake in equity even though it is valid at law. The courts can impose terms on which equitable relief is granted.

Whilst the equitable remedy of rescission is available for common mistake, the remedy is subject to certain bars. The right to rescind may be barred if:

1) the contract has been affirmed;
2) third party rights have intervened;
3) there has been delay;
4) restitution has become impossible.

References

1) [1932] AC 161
2) (1856) 5 HLC 673
3) (1951) 84 CLR 377
4) [1988] 3 All ER 902
5) (1867) LR 2 HL 149
6) (1903) 19 TLR 434
7) [1903] 2 Ch 249
8) (1914) 30 TLR 531
9) [1957] AC 136
10) (1867) LR 2 QB 580
11) (1871) LR 6 QB 597
12) (11th ed) pp225–6

References (continued)

13) [1950] 2 KB 86
14) [1953] 1 QB 646
15) (1947) 177 LT 184
16) [1983] 1 WLR 1315
17) [1950] 1 KB 671
18) [1976] 3 All ER 509
19) [1967] Ch 532
20) [1969] 2 QB 507
21) [1978] 1 WLR 1128

QUESTION 5

Suggested Solution

This question involves a discussion of breach of contract, in particular what amounts to a repudiatory breach and damages. It will be convenient to discuss these matters in connection with the two contracts.

a) The contract between the club and Freddie.

b) The contract between the club and Bill.

a) *The contract between the Red Lion Club and Freddie*

The relevant term in this contract is the undertaking by the Club to provide a selection of 50 records. They appear to have been in breach of that term, by only providing a selection of 30 records. The question is: was the breach of that term a repudiatory breach? The answer to that depends on whether the term is considered a condition or a warranty.

Traditionally contractual terms were divided into conditions and warranties. A condition was regarded as an essential term of the contract, the breach of which entitled an innocent party to treat the contract as repudiated; to terminate it and claim damages. For a breach of warranty the innocent party was not entitled to treat the contract as repudiated; his remedy was limited to a claim in damages. Certain terms do not readily fit into the conventional classification of conditions and warranties. Although the concept was not new the first case to use the expression 'innominate term' was the Court of Appeal decision in *Hong Kong Fir Shipping Co Ltd* v *Kawasaki Kisen Kaisha Ltd* (1). In the case of an innominate term the consequences of the breach depend on whether or not the innocent party has been deprived of the substantial benefit of the transaction. In *Bunge Corporation, New York* v *Tradax Export SA Panama* (2) Lord Scarman said that:

> 'Unless the contract makes it clear, either by express provision or necessary implication arising from its nature, purpose and circumstances ... that a particular stipulation is a condition or only a warranty, it is an innominate term, the remedy for a breach of which depends on the nature, consequences and effect of the breach.'

It is difficult to say whether the relevant term here should be treated as a condition or only as a warranty. It is submitted that it is difficult to argue that the term would be considered a condition. The breach does not appear to deprive Freddie of the substantial benefit of the transaction.

Even if the term is considered a condition, Freddie in order to succeed in his claim would have to establish that the failure to provide the required number of records constitutes a repudiation by the Club of the contract. In *Woodar Investment Development Ltd* v *Wimpey Construction (UK) Ltd* (3) Lord Wilberforce said that:

> '... in considering whether there has been a repudiation by one party, it is necessary to look at his conduct as a whole. Does this indicate an intention to abandon and refuse performance of the contract?'

Freddie then has to establish that the Club has committed an anticipatory breach of contract. If there has been an anticipatory breach of contract by the Club, Freddie is entitled to elect between accepting the breach or holding the Club to the contract: *Frost* v *Knight* (4); *Hochster* v *De la Tour* (5); *White & Carter (Councils) Ltd* v *McGregor* (6). By refusing to perform, and leaving Freddie would appear to have accepted the breach and be entitled to the amount of his fees as damages.

It is submitted, however, that on the present facts it is unlikely that the court would find that there has been an anticipatory breach of contract by the Club.

If that submission is correct, and the Club have not committed an anticipatory breach of contract, it is Freddie who has committed such a breach by refusing to perform and leaving. In the event of Freddie's anticipatory breach it is the Club who is entitled to elect between accepting the breach and affirming the contract.

The Club appears to have accepted the breach. There is nothing to indicate that they have affirmed the contract, on the contrary their conduct in engaging a substitute clearly manifests the intention to accept the breach. On acceptance of the breach the Club is entitled to claim damages – see the cases in connection with acceptance of the breach cited above.

The further question then is for what damages would Freddie be liable? It seems clear that the Club has acted reasonably in mitigating its loss by going on to the market and engaging Super Sally as a substitute performer. The measure of damages would be the difference between the contract price agreed with

Freddie and the fee that the Club was obliged to pay the substitute. Such damages appear to fit within the first limb of *Hadley* v *Baxendale* (7) as arising naturally, that is from the ordinary course of things from the breach.

What is more arguable is whether Freddie can be also held liable for the additional costs incurred by the Company in having to hire the local boys to set up the equipment. This additional loss was caused by the intervening act of a third party, Bill. In accordance with the principles of *Victoria Laundry (Windsor) Ltd* v *Newman Industries Ltd* (8) and *The Heron II* (9) Freddie will be liable for Bill's intervening act if that was reasonably foreseeable, or within Freddie's reasonable contemplation. It can be argued that as Bill was Freddie's mate Bill's action in removing the equipment was something that was 'liable to result'. In that event Freddie will also be liable for these additional costs.

b) *The contract between the Club and Bill*

Bill was not a party to the contract between the Club and Freddie, consequently the rights and obligations of that contract cannot be conferred or imposed on him: *Dunlop Pneumatic Tyre Co Ltd* v *Selfridge & Co Ltd* (10).

Under his contract with the Club, Bill is required to set up the equipment and to remove that equipment after the end of the performance. He in fact removes the equipment before the performance has commenced. He appears therefore to be in breach of an express term of the contract. It can be argued, in the alternative, that there was an implied term in the contract that the equipment was to remain until the conclusion of the performance in accordance with the principles of *The Moorcock* (11) and *Shirlaw* v *Southern Foundries Ltd* (12). As Bill is in breach of contract he is clearly not entitled to demand his fees from the Club. Moreover, he would be liable in damages for the increased costs incurred by the Club in having the equipment reinstated, but the Club does not appear to be contemplating such a claim against him.

Finally, we are informed that the Red Lion Club is a limited company. The relevance of this is that the contractual capacity of a limited liability company is limited by the ultra vires doctrine. Under this doctrine an act which is not authorised by the objects clause of the company is void in law: *Ashbury Railway Carriage & Iron Co* v *Riche* (13). By statute a third party may be able to sue limited companies on ultra vires contracts – s35 Companies Act 1985. Whether a company can itself sue on an ultra vires contract remains uncertain (see *Bell Houses Ltd* v *City Wall Properties Ltd* (14).

There is, however, nothing to indicate that the transactions concerned are ultra vires the company.

References

1) [1962] 2 QB 71
2) [1980] 1 Lloyd's Rep 294
3) [1980] 1 WLR 277
4) (1872) LR 7 Exch 111
5) (1853) 2 E & B 678
6) [1962] AC 413
7) (1854) 9 Exch 341
8) [1949] 2 KB 518
9) [1969] 1 AC 350
10) [1915] AC 79
11) (1889) 14 PD 64
12) [1939] 2 KB 206
13) (1875) LR 7 HL 653
14) [1966] 2 QB 656

QUESTION 6

Suggested Solution

This question requires discussion of the contractual capacity of minors.

Simon, a minor has entered into three contracts. Firstly, for the purchase of a second hand car, secondly, for the purchase of a personal stereo and thirdly, for a set of golf clubs. It is necessary to examine each of these contracts in turn.

a) *The purchase of a second hand car*

A minor is bound by a contract for necessary goods. Necessary goods were defined in the common law as 'such articles as are fit to maintain the particular person in the state, station and degree ... in which he is' (*Peters* v *Fleming* (1)). Section 3(3) of the Sale of Goods Act 1979 defines necessaries as 'goods suitable to the condition in life of the minor ... and to his actual requirements at the time of the sale and delivery'. The onus would be on Finan Motors to prove that the car was not only capable of being a necessary but was so in Simon's particular case: *Nash* v *Inman* (2).

There seems little doubt, in the circumstances, that the car is a necessary. If the car had actually been delivered to Simon he would be bound by the contract. However, Simon has repudiated the contract before the car has been delivered to him and the question is: can the minor be held to an executory contract? This question has not been finally resolved. In *Nash* v *Inman* Fletcher-Moulton LJ held that the minor was liable re, because he had been supplied, and not consensu, because he had contracted. His Lordship held further that a minor was incapable of contracting, and that the law only imposed an obligation upon him to pay if the necessaries had actually been delivered to him. In the same case, however, Buckley LJ held that a contract for necessaries was one that a minor could make. He held that a minor had a limited capacity to contract. The contention that a minor is only bound if the goods have actually been delivered to him is also supported by the definition of necessaries in the Sale of Goods Act quoted above. Under s3(2) of the same Act the minor is only obliged to pay a reasonable price for the necessaries, which may not be the contract price.

These statutory definitions suggest that a minor is only bound if he has actually been supplied with the necessary goods, and that the minor would not be bound by an executory contract. However, there is authority to the contrary. In *Roberts* v *Gray* (3) the defendant, who was a minor, desired to become a professional billiard player and made a contract with Roberts under which the parties agreed to accompany each other on a world tour and to play matches together. Roberts expended a great deal of time and trouble and incurred certain liabilities in the course of preparing for the contract. Gray repudiated the contract while it was still largely executory and Roberts obtained damages for breach of contract. In the Court of Appeal Hamilton LJ said:

> 'I am unable to appreciate why a contract which is in itself binding, because it is a contract for necessaries ..., can cease to be binding merely because it is executory ... If the Contract is binding at all it must be binding for all such remedies as are appropriate of it.'

In Cheshire, Fifoot & Furmston's *Law of Contract* (4) it is observed that the contract in *Roberts* v *Gray* was more closely analagous to beneficial contracts of service, which are binding even though not completely executed. It is also observed that all the authorities relied upon by the court in *Roberts* v *Gray* concern beneficial contracts of service. Treitel (5) has the view that it is difficult to justify the distinction between necessary goods and beneficial contracts of service. Treitel considers that the reasons for holding a minor liable and for limiting his liability are the same in both cases.

The position is therefore still open to argument. However it is submitted that Treitel's view is the better one. If that is so, Simon would be bound by the contract and therefore liable in damages to Finan Motors for breach of contract. It is clear that the suppliers could not obtain an order for specific performance against him.

b) *The purchase of the stereo*

It seems clear that the stereo is not a necessary. Whilst Simon, therefore, would not be bound by the contract the other party, General Trading plc is bound by the contract: *Bruce* v *Warwick* (6). General Trading plc appear to be in breach of contract. More particularly they are in breach of s14(2) of the Sale of Goods Act – the implied condition that the goods supplied under the contract are of merchantable quality. (The provision is the Infants Relief Act 1874 which made certain contracts with minors 'absolutely void' has now been repealed by the Minors Contract Act 1987.) General Trading plc are therefore liable in damages to Simon. They would therefore be liable for the cost of the tape that has been damaged: such damage would be reasonably foreseeable, see *Hadley* v *Baxendale* (7), etc. We are informed that the tape was of great sentimental value. Whether this would increase the damages available to Simon is however doubtful. It is not immediately apparent that such increased damages would have been reasonably foreseeable. It could be argued, though, that as General Trading plc could have foreseen the kind of damage, they are not absolved from liability merely because they could not foresee the extent of the damage: *H Parsons (Livestock) Ltd* v *Uttley Ingham & Co Ltd* (8). It is also possible that Simon's claim for the loss of an article of sentimental value is closely akin to claiming damages for distress. In *Bliss* v *South East Thames Regional Health Authority* (9) Dillon LJ stated that damages for distress were limited to cases 'where the contract which has been broken was itself a contract to provide peace of mind or freedom from distress.' A similar view was taken by the Court of Appeal in *Hayes* v *James & Charles Dodd* (10). It does not appear that the purchase of the stereo was such a contract and that therefore a claim in respect of the sentimental value of the tape could not be supported, as the damages would be too remote.

As the contract for the stereo has already been performed Simon cannot recover back the money he paid for it: *Corpe* v *Overton* (11).

c) *The purchase of the golf clubs*
It seems clear that the golf clubs are not necessaries. The supplier can therefore not claim either the contract price or a reasonable price from Simon. Simon can, however, be held liable to restore the golf clubs to General Trading plc. Such liability was imposed in equity before the Minors Contract Act 1987. Section 3(1) of the Act now gives the court a discretion to order the minor to transfer to the adult party any property acquired by the minor under a contract which was not enforceable against him. There seems to be no reason why the court would not exercise its discretion in favour of General Trading plc and order Simon to transfer the golf clubs back to them.

References

1) (1840) 6 M & W 42
2) [1908] 2 KB 1
3) [1913] 1 KB 520
4) *Law of Contract* (11th ed) p415
5) *The Law of Contract* (7th ed) p420
6) (1815) 6 Taunt 341
7) (1854) 9 Exch 341
8) [1978] QB 791
9) [1987] ICR 700
10) (1988) The Times 14 July
11) (1833) 10 Bing 252

QUESTION 7

Suggested Solution

This question involves discussion of a number of issues: the rules relating to sufficiency of consideration; duress; and promisory estoppel. There are two contracts in question, one between Giles and Illtyd, the other between Giles and Peter. These two contracts will be discussed in turn.

The contract between Giles and Illtyd

The contract between Giles and Illtyd is for the latter to perform the construction work for the fixed price of £3,000. Illtyd then discovers that certain additional work is necessary and Giles has agreed to pay an additional £500. Two matters arise: whether there was any consideration for the promise to make the additional payment and; whether the promise to pay was exacted by duress.

The question here is whether, in continuing the work, Illtyd was performing no more than an existing contractual duty, or whether he was now performing something over and above his original contractual obligations. It may well be that Illtyd undertook, in constructing the patio and fish pond, to do whatever was necessary to complete that task, and that if the removal of the cannon was necessary, it was part of his original obligation. If Illtyd is performing no more than his existing contractual duty, there is authority for the view that this is not sufficient consideration: *Stilk* v *Myrick* (1); *North Ocean Shipping Co* v *Hyundai Construction Co (The Atlantic Baron)* (2). If the removal of the cannon was within Illtyd's existing contractual obligations, then no fresh consideration has been furnished for Giles' promise to pay the additional £500. That promise would, therefore, be unenforceable.

It is, however, possible that Illtyd is now performing some extra task, in which case there has been fresh consideration for the promise to pay the £500: *Hartley* v *Ponsonby* (3). I shall proceed on that assumption.

If there has been fresh consideration, the further question remains as to whether the promise to pay the additional amount was obtained by duress. Illtyd threatens to break his contract with Giles unless Giles pays the additional amount. There is now substantial authority for the proposition that a threat to break a contract constitutes economic duress: *Occidental Worldwide Investment Corp* v *Skibs A/S Avanti (The Sibeon and The Sibotre)* (4); *North Ocean Shipping Co* (above); *B & S Contracts* v *Victor Green Publications Ltd* (5). In *Pao On* v *Lau Yiu Long* (6), Lord Scarman stated that four criteria would have to be considered in order to decide whether or not there had been economic duress. These criteria were: i) whether the victim had protested, ii) whether the victim had an alternative legal remedy, iii) whether the victim had had independent legal advice, and iv) whether he took steps to avoid the transaction, after the duress had ceased.

The effect of economic duress is that the victim can have the contract set aside and may be entitled to claim damages in tort.

In it not clear, on the facts presented, whether or not Giles could establish that he had been induced to make the promise to pay the additonal amount by virtue of economic duress, having regard to the criteria set out above. However the courts have shown increasing readiness to recognise the concept of economic duress, and if Giles can establish, in particular, that he had no choice but to submit to Illtyd's demand, then he may well succeed in establishing economic duress. See the recent case of *Atlas Express Ltd* v *Kafco (Importers and Distributors) Ltd* (7).

The contract between Giles and Peter

In agreeing that Giles need only pay the interest on the loan and not the instalments, Peter has promised to suspend his contractual rights. At common law Peter's promise to suspend his contractual rights is unenforceable because there has been no consideration for that promise. This common law principle laid down in *Pinnel's Case* (8) was affirmed by the House of Lords in *Foakes* v *Beer*: (9).

The common law rule has, however, been modified by the equitable doctrine of promissory estoppel. This doctrine derives from the decision of the House of Lords in *Huges* v *Metropolitan Railway Co* (10). It was developed further by Denning J (as he then was) in obiter dicta in *Central London Property Trust Ltd* v *High Trees House Ltd* (11). Although the doctrine of promissory estoppel has been criticised as being inconsistent with *Foakes* v *Beer* (above) and with *Jordan* v *Money* (12), it has become established. It has been recognised by the House of Lords in *Tool Metal Manufacturing Co Ltd* v *Tungsten Electric Co Ltd* (13) and by the privy council in *FA Ajayi* v *RT Briscoe (Nigeria) Ltd* (14). The essence of the doctrine is that when one party to a contract promises, in the absence of fresh consideration, not to enforce his rights, an equity will be raised in favour of the other party, which will estop the party who made the promise from going back on it.

In order to determine whether the equity operates in Giles' favour certain aspects have to be considered.

1) In order for the doctrine to operate Peter must have made an unequivocal promise: *Woodhouse AC Israel Cocoa Ltd* v *Nigerian Produce Marketing Co* (15). He appears to have done so.
2) The further requirement is that Giles has acted on Peter's promise. It has to be shown that there has been reliance on the promise. The balance of authority suggests that it is not necessary to show that Giles has acted to his detriment: *W J Alan & Co Ltd* v *El Nasr Export & Import Co* (16); *Societe Italo-Belge* v *Palm Oils (The Post Chaser)* (17). (There is a suggestion to the contrary in the obiter dicta of Nourse LJ in *Goldsworthy* v *Brickell* (18)). It is, however, necessary for Giles to show that as a result of Peter's promise he was led to act differently from the way he would otherwise have done. It is not clear, from the present facts, whether this is so.
3) It does not appear that Peter's promise was exacted by any form of pressure as in *D & C Builders Ltd* v *Rees* (19). It could not be suggested, therefore, that it would not be inequitable to allow Peter to resile from his promise.
4) The further aspect that has to be examined is whether Peter's promise is extinctive or merely suspensive of his rights. In *FA Ajayi* v *RT Briscoe (Nigeria) Ltd* (above) Lord Hodson stated that the promisor can resile from his promise on giving the promisee a reasonable opportunity of resuming his position. It is only when the promisee cannot resume his former position that the promise becomes irrecovable. This suggests that when Giles finds a new job Peter can demand the resumption of the payments of the agreed instalments, on giving Giles reasonable notice to do so. There is no direct authority as to whether or not Peter would be entitled to demand immediate payment of the outstanding arrears of capital. Lord Denning has stated extra judicially that the rights to the arrear payments in *High Trees* had been extinguished. This does not mean that Peter has abandoned any portion of the capital sum due to him, but that he has promised to extend the period of repayment. He might not be able to resile from this promise.

The difficulty for Giles is to establish that he relied on Peter's promise. If he cannot do so the doctrine of promisory estoppel cannot operate in his favour. If Giles can establish reliance, he is advised that Peter cannot resile from his promise until he (Giles) has found a new job. When Giles obtains a new job Peter can demand resumption of payment of the agreed instalments until the full capital sum has been paid off. Peter would not be able to claim immediate payment of the outstanding arrears of capital.

References

1) (1809) 2 Camp 317
2) [1979] QB 705
3) (1857) 7 E & B 872
4) [1976] 1 Lloyd's Rep 293
5) [1984] ICR 419
6) [1980] AC 614
7) [1989] 1 All ER 641
8) (1602) 5 Co Rep 117a
9) (1884) 9 App Cas 605
10) (1877) 2 App Cas 439
11) [1947] 1 KB 130
12) (1854) 5 HLC 185
13) [1955] 1 WLR 761
14) [1964] 1 WLR 132
15) [1972] AC 741
16) [1972] 2 QB 189
17) [1981] 2 Lloyd's Rep 695
18) [1987] 1 All ER 853
19) [1966] 2 QB 617

UNIVERSITY OF LONDON
INTERMEDIATE EXAMINATION IN LAWS 1989
for External Students

ELEMENTS OF THE LAW OF CONTRACT

Tuesday, 13 June: 10.00 am to 1.00 pm

Answer *FOUR* of the following SEVEN questions.

1 In January 1989 X privately advertised his house for sale for £100,000. J and his wife, M, who was expecting a baby in March 1989, came to inspect the House. X informed J that the house was in 'first class condition throughout' and that X had just installed a new gas central heating system that was safe and efficient and that J need not worry about the house being cold for his new baby. When J asked if the house was noisy X replied that it was always quiet. J agreed to buy the house.

After living in the house for only a few days J and M discovered that their neighbours were awful and fought all the time. J and M could hear these fights. Soon after J smelt gas and it was discovered that the gas central heating was dangerous and needed to be replaced at a cost of £2,000. J was forced to move his family to a hotel for a week at a cost of £300 while the central heating was replaced. While at the hotel J heard that the local authority had just granted planning permission for the house next door to be used as a day centre for homeless teenagers. The value of J's house immediately fell by £30,000.

Advise J.

2 Alban is a baker and confectioner. One of his most famous specialities is a 'golden sun cake' which he makes according to a secret recipe known to him alone. A vital ingredient for the cake is a liqueur produced only in Ruritania. In March this year Alban concluded a contract with Tessbury plc, a supermarket chain, under which he agreed to supply 5,000 golden sun cakes a week for a period of 3 years commencing on June 1 at a price of £2 each. Alban told Tessbury that the cakes contained Ruritanian liqueur, so that this could be stated on the packets. Tessbury paid Alban £2,000 on the signing of the contract and agreed to pay monthly in arrears for cakes delivery. During

April and May Alban spent £8,000 extending his bakery premises and installing new ovens in order to ensure that he could produce enough cakes to fulfil the Tessbury order.

On June 2, when Alban tried to obtain fresh supplies of the Ruritanian liqueur, he discovered that the failure of the spring rains had brought production of the liqueur to a standstill and that it would be unobtainable until June 1990 at the earliest. When Tessbury heard this they wrote to Alban cancelling the contract and demanding the return of the £2,000.

Advise Alban.

Would your answer be different if Ruritanian liqueur was still available but the price had risen to such an extent that it would now cost Alban £3 to make each cake?

3 On Tuesday A, a writer who works from home, advertised his car number plate 'GBH 1' in the local paper for £600. H on seeing the advertisement called at A's house on the same day to see the number plate. After discussion, A offered to sell the number plate to H for £500. H stated that he would need some time to think it over but that if A had heard nothing from H by Wednesday evening he could assume that H had bought it. A replied that this arrangement was fine by him.

At 3pm that afternoon Z telephoned A and offered to buy A's plate for £1,200. A immediately accepted Z's offer and telephoned H. As H was out, A left a message on H's answering machine revoking his original offer. Unknown to H and A, the answering machine was broken and did not record the message. A however was still worried about the situation and tried to ring H again at 6 pm that evening. This time A spoke to W, H's wife, and told her that the number plate had been sold. W said that she expected H home at 6.30 pm and would pass the message on to him then. Unknown to A or W, H had already decided to buy the number plate and had faxed his acceptance to A's home at 5.15 pm. A did not read H's acceptance until 6.30 pm. H came home at 7.15 pm and W then gave him the message from A.

Advise A.

4 'The rules on remoteness of damage and mitigation in contract are simply instruments which courts use in their attempt to legitimise the arbitrary damages awards that they make.'

Discuss.

5 P and Q are rival art dealers who live in the same town. In August 1988, while P was on holiday in Spain, he acquired what

he honestly believed was a valuable painting by Goya. On returning home he offered the painting for sale. Q, after having viewed the painting and also believing it to be a Goya, sent his agent, W, to buy the painting, instructing him to pose as Sir Charles Trevelyan. P sold the painting to W for £250,000, pleased at last that he was attracting wealthy clientele. Q subsequently resold the painting for £300,000 to S who also believed it was a Goya. Last month all the parties discovered that they were mistaken and that the painting is in fact a missing part of Guernica by Picasso and that the art world has been searching for this painting for years. It is worth £2,000,000.

Advise P.

6 'The unsatisfactory nature of the doctrine of restraint of trade is due to the inherent contradiction between it and the idea of freedom of contract.'

Discuss.

7 Cecil, a travel agent, ordered a word processor from Beta Ltd for his office. He signed the order form, which provided that Beta Ltd would replace or repair free of charge any goods sold by them which proved to be defective within nine months of purchase but were otherwise not to be under any liability whatsoever for loss or damage caused by defects in the goods.

After Cecil had used the word processor for a month he was so pleased with it that he bought a similar one for his personal use at home. The order form contained the same provision as before concerning Beta Ltd's liability for defective goods.

Shortly afterwards the word processor in Cecil's office developed a fault which caused the loss of the entire records of holiday bookings for July 1989. Cecil had to hire extra staff to do the work of reconfirming the bookings. Soon afterwards the word processor in Cecil's home suffered an electrical breakdown. Cecil received a severe electric shock and was unable to work for six weeks.

Advise Cecil.

QUESTION 1

Suggested Solution

X made a number of oral statements to J prior to the sale of the house. The statement that the house was in 'first class condition throughout' appears to be a 'mere puff' and is without legal effect. A vague, eulogistic statement is not actionable: *Dimmock* v *Hallett* (1).

The further statements with regard to the central heating and that the house was quiet do appear to be more precise statements of fact. It must first be considered whether these statements are contractual terms or 'mere' representations. The question is one of the intention of the parties deduced from all the evidence: *Heilbut, Symons & Co* v *Buckleton* (2); *Oscar Chess Ltd* v *Williams* (3); *Dick Bentley Productions Ltd* v *Harold Smith (Motors) Ltd* (4). The court will employ various criteria in determining whether a statement is a contractual term or a representation. One of these is that if the contract is subsequently reduced to writing, and the statement is not incorporated in the written document, this would indicate that the statement was not intended to be a contractual term: *Routledge* v *McKay* (5). The contract for the sale of the house would have been in writing. The statements are, moreover, not couched in contractual terms and it is submitted, therefore, that they must be dealt with on the basis that they are, if anything, representations.

For a statement to amount to an actionable misrepresentation it must be:

i) one of fact;
ii) false;
iii) addressed to the party misled; and
iv) a substantial factor in inducing the representee to enter into the contract.

The statement that X had installed a new central heating system that was safe appears to meet all these requirements. It is, therefore, an actionable misrepresentation.

The statement that the house was always quiet is perhaps more questionable. It might be considered to be a statement not of fact, but of opinion. But X must be presumed to have known of the conduct of his neighbours and he could not reasonably held such an opinion. Contrast the case of *Bisset v Wilkinson* (6) with the cases of *Smith* v *Land and House Property Corporation* (7) and *Esso Petroleum Co Ltd* v *Mardon* (8). In the former case the particular statement was merely an opinion and did not, therefore, amount to a representation: in the latter two cases because the parties concerned were deemed to have knowledge of the particular facts the 'opinions' were regarded as representations. It seems that the statement here would be regarded as a representation in view of X's knowledge. It clearly meets the other requirements for an actionable misrepresentation.

It is not clear what the relevance is of the of the local authority having granted permission for the house next door to be used as described. It is not evident that X was aware that this was going to – or might – happen. Even if he were so aware, the failure to disclose this would not of itself constitute a misrepresentation. Silence does not amount to a misrepresentation, but X's failure to disclose the eventuality would strengthen the view that his statement that the house was quiet is an actionable misrepresentation.

As there are actionable misrepresentations what must be now considered are the remedies available to J.

Rescission is an available remedy whether the misrepresentation is fraudulent, negligent or innocent. The fact that the contract has been performed is not a bar to rescission – s1(b) Misrepresentation Act 1967. Nor do there appear to be any equitable bars to rescission. Under s2(2) of the Act the court has a discretion to award damages in lieu of rescission (where the misrepresentation is otherwise than fraudulent), but there is nothing to indicate such an exercise of the discretion here.

The further possible remedy is damages. This depends on the nature of the misrepresentation.

A remedy in damages is always available for fraudulent misrepresentation. But the onus of proving fraud is on the party alleging it. It is a difficult burden to discharge. In *Derry* v *Peek* (9) Lord Herschell said that fraud is proved when it is shown that a false representation has been made knowingly, or without belief in its truth, or recklessly, careless whether it be true or false. It is not to possible to advise J that he will be able to establish fraud on X's part. If he were able to do so then X would be liable to compensate him for all the losses flowing directly from the misrepresentations. If the decision of the local authority which resulted in the fall in value of the property could be laid at X's door then X would be liable for that loss in addition to his liability for the cost of repairing the central heating: *Doyle* v *Olby (Ironmongers) Ltd* (10).

However, if J cannot establish fraud, and it is doubtful whether he can do so, he should be advised to pursue a claim for damages under s2(1) of the Act. This sub-section provides that where a party has suffered loss as a result of a misrepresentation and the representor would be liable in damages if the representation had been made fraudulently, then the representor will also be so liable unless he proves that he had reasonable ground to believe and did believe up to the time the contract was made that the facts represented were true. This shifts the burden of proof to X, and it is difficult to see how he could discharge this burden. The measure of damages under s2(1) is the tortious measure – see the judgment of Mervyn Davies J in *Sharneyford Supplies Ltd* v *Edge* (11). This means that J would be able to recover his expenses, the cost of the new central heating, but not his loss of bargain, the fall in value of the property.

There does not appear to be any special relationship between X and J which would justify an action for negligent misstatement under *Hedley Byrne & Co Ltd* v *Heller & Partners Ltd* (12). In any event, as the basis of damages would, in such an action be, the same as that under s2(1) this would not take the matter any further.

If X is able to discharge the onus of proof imposed on him by s2(1) then the misrepresentations would be wholly innocent and he would not be liable in damages. But it is submitted that this is unlikely.

References

1) (1866) 2 Ch App 21
2) [1913] AC 30
3) [1957] 1 WLR 370
4) [1965] 1 WLR 623
5) [1954] 1 WLR 615
6) [1927] AC 177
7) (1884) 28 Ch D 7
8) [1976] 1 QB 801
9) (1889) 15 App Cas 337
10) [1969] 2 QB 158
11) [1985] 1 All ER 976
12) [1964] AC 465

QUESTION 2

Suggested Solution

What is at issue here is whether the contract between Alban and Tessbury has been frustrated.

The doctrine of frustration applies when a change of circumstances renders a contract physically or commercially impossible to perform or the circumstances transform the performance into something radically different from that which the parties undertook when they entered into the contract.

Prior to 1863 contractual obligations were regarded as absolute: *Paradine* v *Jane* (1). The doctrine was first recognised in English law in *Taylor* v *Caldwell* (2) where the subject matter of the contract – a music hall – was destroyed by fire. Blackburn J held that the effect of the destruction of the subject matter was to discharge the parties from their further obligations under the contract. The basis of the doctrine of frustration in that case was the implied term theory: the parties had contracted on the basis of the continued existence of the subject matter.

The implied term theory has now been largely rejected by the courts and has been superseded by the 'radical change in obligations' test. This was first formulated by Lord Radcliffe in *Davis Contractors Ltd* v *Fareham Urban District Council* (3) in the following words:

> '... frustration occurs whenever the law recognises that without default of either party a contractual obligation has become incapable of being performed because the circumstances in which performance is called for would render it a thing radically different from that which was undertaken by the contract. *Non haec in foedera veni.* It was not this that I promised to do.'

In two subsequent decisions of the House of Lords this test has been approved and adopted: *National Carriers Ltd* v *Panalpina (Northern) Ltd* (4); *Pioneer Shipping* v *BTP Tioxide (The Nema)* (5).

However the doctrine of frustration will only apply in limited circumstances. The mere fact that the contract has become more expensive or onerous to perform will not be sufficient for the doctrine to be invoked. In *Davis* the particular circumstances caused considerable delay in the performance and caused the contractors considerable additional expense but this was held to be a long way from a case of frustration. In *Ocean Tramp Tankers Corporation* v *V.O. Sovfracht, The Eugenia* (6) the unforeseen circumstances again caused delay and extra expense in the performance of the contract but this did not warrant finding that the contract had been frustrated. See also *Tsakiroglou & Co Ltd* v *Noblee Thorl GmbH* (7).

In the present problem an event has occurred without the fault of either party and which was not provided for in the contract. This will cause a delay of at least a year in the performance of the contract which is of three years' duration. It has been recognise that a delay can be so long as to put an end in a commercial sense to the venture entered upon by the parties: *Jackson* v *Union Marine Insurance Co Ltd* (8). It is submitted that, in the present context, the delay of a year does have this effect, and does make the contract 'a radically different thing' from that which the parties entered into. Thus the contract has been frustrated.

What must now been considered is the effect of this. At common law, as has been noted, the effect of frustration is to discharge the parties from their further obligations. With regard to the commitments of Alban and Tessbury prior to the frustrating event one must turn to the provisions of the Law Reform (Frustrated Contracts) Act 1943.

Section 1(2) of the Act provides that the £2,000 paid by Tessbury is recoverable. There is, however, a proviso to this. Where a party who has received a payment has incurred expenses for the purpose of performing the contract the court has the discretion to allow him to retain the whole or part of the sums paid, not being an amount in excess of the expenses incurred. Alban has incurred expenses of £8,000, but his recovery for this expenditure is limited by the amount paid or payable before the frustrating event. £2,000 had been paid by Tessbury, but no further sums were payable when the contract was frustrated. It would appear, therefore, that the court might well allow Alban to retain the £2,000, but the loss of the additional expenditure will fall on him.

Under s1(3) of the Act provision is made for the award of a 'just sum' where one party has obtained a valuable benefit before the contract was discharged. The benefit must be valued at the date of the frustration: *BP Exploration Co (Libya) Ltd* v *Hunt* (9). In this problem no benefit has been obtained by either party at the date of frustration, so s1(3) does not apply.

Alban is therefore advised that the contract with Tessbury has been discharged by frustration, but that he should resist the demand for the return of the £2,000, relying on the proviso to s1(2) of the Act.

It remains to consider what the position would be if the Ruritanian liqueur was still available, but the cost had now risen to the extent stated.

As set out above the fact that a contract has become more expensive to perform is not a sufficient indication of frustration. Treitel (10) quotes authorities in the United States to the effect that a 'marked increase in cost' or a price increase 'well beyond the normal range' might constitute a frustrating event. But the tendency in the United States has been to widen the scope of the doctrine of frustration. In contrast the House of Lords held in *British Movietone News Ltd* v *London and District Cinemas* (11) that 'a wholly abnormal rise or fall in prices' would not affect the bargain.

In view of the restrictive attitude of our courts to the doctrine of frustration it seems that Alban would be held to the contract despite the substantial increase in price of the liqueur. As this would involve him in having to carry out the contract at a considerable loss it may be that a court would hold that this entailed a radical change in the obligations. But Alban could not be advised with confidence that a court would take this view.

References

1) (1647) Aleyn 26
2) (1863) 3 B & S 826
3) [1956] AC 696
4) [1981] AC 675
5) [1981] 3 WLR 292
6) [1964] 2 QB 226
7) [1962] AC 93
8) (1874) LR 10 CP 125
9) [1979] 1WLR 783
10) *The Law of Contract* (7th ed) p678
11) [1952] AC 166

QUESTION 3

Suggested Solution

This question involves discussion of the rules relating to offer, the revocation of an offer and acceptance.

It is scarcely necessary to emphasise that the advertisement which A places in the local paper is not an offer, but an invitation to treat: *Partridge* v *Crittenden* (1). However A has made a clear offer to H to sell him the number plate for £500. The question is: has H accepted the offer, or has A revoked the offer before he did so?

H informs A that if he (A) heard nothing from him by Wednesday evening he could assume that H had bought it. A agrees to this. An offeror cannot impose silence as a form of acceptance on an offeree: *Felthouse* v *Bindley* (2). It is, however, arguable that an offeror can waive communication of acceptance, and that he will consequently be contractually bound by the offeree's silence. Treitel (3) suggests that the object of the rule that the offeror cannot impose silence as acceptance is to protect the offeree from the trouble and expense of having to reject the offer. The rule, he says, should not be invoked for the protection of the offeror. It seems possible that, in the absence of further communication, the contract between A and H would have been concluded 'by Wednesday evening', if this time could be more precisely defined. But this is perhaps a doubtful proposition. It is clear, however, that A's offer was to be kept open at least until the Wednesday evening.

An offer can be revoked at any time before acceptance: this does not require further argument. But the revocation must be actually communicated to the offeree before he has accepted the offer: *Byrne Co* v *Leon van Tienhoven* (4). Merely selling the number plate to Z does not constitute revocation: *Adams* v *Lindsell* (5). A has purported to revoke his offer. When, if at all, has that revocation been communicated?

A attempts to inform H that he has revoked the offer, by leaving a message on H's answering machine, but for the reasons given H does not receive this message. There is no clear authority as to when a message left on an answering machine is deemed to be communicated. It might be argued that the message is deemed to be received either when it is placed on the machine, or perhaps when it should have been heard in the normal course of events. The latter proposition is probably more justifiable and could be supported by the decision in *The Brimnes* (6), where a telex message was deemed to have been received during ordinary business hours; although that case that case was concerned with the termination of a contract, not its formation.

In the present situation H does not receive the message – it is presumed through no fault of his own. Moreover there is no indication that he could have expected to receive the message at any particular time. On the contrary he was not anticipating any message of revocation at all. He assumed, and was entitled to assume by A's concurrence, that the contract would be concluded unless he advised A that he did not wish to buy the plate. In dealing with the problem of instantaneous communication in *Entores Ltd* v *Miles Far East Corporation* (7) Denning LJ (as he then was) said that 'if there should be a case where the offeror without any fault on his part does not receive the the message of acceptance – yet the sender of it reasonably believes it has got home when it has not – then I think there is no contract.' If one adapts that dictum to the present facts by substituting the message of revocation from the offeror for the message of acceptance from the offeree, one is again led to the conclusion that there has been no effective revocation of the offer at this stage.

A makes a further attempt to revoke his offer by again telephoning H. He informs W, H's wife that the offer has, in effect, been revoked. There is nothing to suggest that W had authority to receive the information. At most she might have had authority to transmit the message. In *Henthorn* v *Fraser* (8) it was held that the effect of giving a message of acceptance to an agent depended on the scope of the agent's authority. This must also apply to a message of revocation.

The revocation is, then, only communicated when H actually receives the message. *Dickinson* v *Dodds* (9) is authority for the proposition that the revocation need not be communicated directly by the offeror. But H only receives the message at 7.15pm. It is, it is submitted, irrelevant that W expected H to be home at 6.30 pm and said she would pass the message to him at that time.

At 6.30 pm at the latest H's acceptance of the offer had been communicated to A. If the submission is correct that the revocation of the offer was only communicated at 7.15pm then it was ineffective, a contract having been concluded at the prior time.

Assuming, for the sake of argument, that W had authority to inform A that H would receive the message at 6.30pm, or that H is estopped from denying this, it must be considered whether H's acceptance could be deemed to have been communicated earlier than the time at which he read it.

H faxed his acceptance to A's home at 5.15pm. We are informed that A works from home so H appears to be justified in employing this method of communication. The caveat has already been entered that the case of *The Brimnes* (above) was concerned with the termination of a contract, not its formation. But if the approach in that case can be applied here it remains to consider whether A could be deemed to have received the message of acceptance during normal working hours and whether this would be prior to the time when he actually read it. This is perhaps speculative, but must be regarded as a possibility.

For the reasons given, however, I have concluded that, as H was not made aware of the revocation until 7.15pm, A is contractually bound to H and will be liable to him for breach of contract.

References

1) [1968] 1 WLR 1204
2) (1862) 11 CB (NS) 869
3) *The Law of Contract* (7th ed) pp27–28
4) (1880) 5 CPD 344
5) (1818) 1 B & Ald 681
6) [1975] QB 929
7) [1955] 2 QB 327
8) [1892] 2 Ch 27
9) (1876) 2 Ch D 463

QUESTION 4

Suggested Solution

The proposition contained in this quotation would not gain universal acceptance. It can be argued that damages awards appear to be arbitrary because the courts attempt to achieve a balance between two objectives. On the one hand they seek to compensate the plaintiff for the loss he has suffered, on the other hand they seek to avoid visiting the defendant with liability for loss that he could not have contemplated or loss that could, with reasonable prudence, have been avoided.

'The rule of the common law is that where a party sustains a loss by breach of contract, he is, so far as money can do it, to be placed in the same position as if the contract had been performed.' – *Robinson* v *Harman* (1). This is an expression of the first objective. It must be noted that the courts will, in awarding damages, avoid placing the plaintiff in a better position than he would have been in if the contract had been fully performed: *C & P Haulage (A Firm)* v *Middleton* (2).

The rule that the plaintiff should be put in the position he would have been in if the contract had been performed would, if logically pursued, afford the plaintiff a complete indemnity for all loss resulting from a breach, however improbable or unpredictable. In order, therefore, to meet the second objective the rule is subject to the limitation that the damages must not be too remote. Accordingly the courts have developed a further rule to limit the liability of the defendant to loss which the law regards as sufficiently proximate.

This further rule found expression in the judgment of Alderson B in *Hadley* v *Baxendale* (3) where it was said to consist of two limbs. To be recoverable the damages should be such as may fairly and reasonably be considered as either arising naturally, that is according to the usual course of things, from such breach of contract itself, or such as may reasonably be supposed to have been in the contemplation of both parties, at the time they made the contract, as the probable result of the breach of it.

In *Victoria Laundry (Windsor) Ltd* v *Newman Industries Ltd* (4) Asquith LJ re-formulated the rule in *Hadley* v *Baxendale* in the following propositions:

i) the plaintiff is only entitled to recover loss which was at the time of the contract reasonably forseeable as liable to result from the breach;

ii) what was reasonably foreseeable depends on the knowledge then possessed by the parties;

iii) knowledge is of two types, imputed and actual. Imputed knowledge is the knowledge that everyone, as a reasonable person, is taken to have of the ordinary course of things. Actual knowledge is knowledge which the contract-breaker actually possesses of special circumstances outside the ordinary course of things, which make additional loss liable to result;

iv) the contract-breaker need not have actually asked himself what loss was liable to result, it is sufficient that as a reasonable man he would have done so;

v) the plaintiff need not prove that it would be foreseen that the loss would necessarily result from the breach, it was sufficient that it was a 'serious possibility' or a 'real danger'. This could be expressed as 'liable to result'.

These propositions were considered by the House of Lords in *The Heron II* (5). Their Lordships approved them in general terms, but they held that the test was not one of 'reasonable foreseeability' – which was the test in tort – but one of 'reasonable contemplation' which term denoted a higher degree of probability. The distinction between tests in contract and in tort might be regarded as arbitrary. In *H Parsons (Livestock) Ltd* v *Uttley Ingham & Co Ltd* (6) both Lord Denning MR and Scarman LJ (as he then was) expressed the view that it was absurd that the test for remoteness of damage should differ according to the legal classification of the cause of action. Lord Denning was also of the opinion that different tests applied to physical damage (damage to person or property) and economic (deprivation of profit) loss. But Scarman and Orr LJJ rejected this distinction.

In this case the Court of Appeal re-affirmed the principle that, if physical injury or damage is within the contemplation of the parties, recovery is not limited because the degree of such damage could not have been anticipated. In *Wroth* v *Tyler* (7) Megarry J applied a similar principle with respect to economic loss.

It could be suggested that somewhat arbitrary limits have been defined as to the damage recoverable. In *Addis* v *Gramaphone Co Ltd* (8) the House of Lords held that damages could not be recovered for loss of reputation or injury to feelings. This limitation has more recently been re-affirmed by the Court of Appeal in *Bliss* v *South*

East Thames Regional Health Authority (9). It appears, however, that in certain types of contract damages may be awarded for distress occasioned by the breach of contract: *Jarvis* v *Swan's Tours Ltd* (10); *Jackson* v *Horizon Holidays Ltd* (11). But there is a limit to damages for distress. In *Bliss* Dillon LJ said that such damages should be confined to cases where the contract which has been broken was itself a contract to provide peace of mind or freedom from distress.

The plaintiff's recovery of damages might also be limited by the duty imposed on him by the common law to mitigate his loss. He must take reasonable steps to minimise his loss; furthermore he must refrain from taking unreasonable steps that increase his loss.

If the plaintiff fails to take reasonable steps to minimise his loss he cannot recover anything for the extra loss arising from his failure. What is usually required of the plaintiff is that he should seek a substitute contract. If a seller fails to deliver the goods the buyer has the duty to go into the market and purchase substitute goods. The plaintiff is required only to take *reasonable* steps. Where there are two reasonable courses of action open to the plaintiff either will be sufficient to comply with his duty to mitigate: *Gebruder Metelmann GmbH & Co* v *NBR (London) Ltd* (12). The plaintiff is not required to take risks in order to mitigate his loss: *Pilkington* v *Wood* (13). An employee who is wrongfully dismissed is under the duty to seek alternative employment. Again only reasonable steps are required of the employee. He need not accept an offer of a job at a reduced status: *Yetton* v *Eastwood Froy Ltd* (14).

The plaintiff must avoid taking unreasonable steps in attempting to mitigate which would actually increase his loss. Thus he should not incur expense in attempting to tender performance after it has become clear that the defendant will reject it.

The benefits a plaintiff obtains as a result of his mitigation must be taken into account in assessing his damages, even if he acquires these benefits as a result of steps which he was not required to take: *British Westinghouse Co* v *Underground Electric Rys Co of London* (15).

In conclusion it is submitted that whilst there are possibly arbitrary distinctions drawn and anomalous limits set in the rules relating to remoteness of damage and mitigation, it is not justifiable to characterise these rules as merely instruments to justify the awards that the courts make.

References

1) (1848) 1 Ex 850
2) [1983] 1 WLR 1461
3) (1854) 9 Exch 341

References (continued)

4) [1949] 2 KB 528
5) [1969] AC 350
6) [1978] QB 791
7) [1974] Ch 30
8) [1909] AC 488
9) [1985] ICR 700
10) [1973] 1 QB 233
11) [1975] 1 WLR 1468
12) [1984] 1 Lloyd's Rep 614
13) [1953] Ch 770
14) [1967] 1 WLR 104
15) [1912] AC 673

QUESTION 5

Suggested Solution

This question involves discussion of two areas of mistake; mistake as to identity, and mutual mistake.

The mistake as to identity

P sells the painting to W (Q's agent) in the mistaken belief that the buyer is Sir Charles Trevelyan. It seems clear that P has been induced to sell the painting to W by a fraudulent misrepresentation. Whilst the remedy of rescission may be available for such misrepresentation, in this case a third party has acquired rights to the painting, and this is a bar to rescission. (Whether P has an action for damages in the tort of deceit against Q or his agent is beyond the scope of this question.)

It will not therefore avail P merely to establish that the contract was voidable. P would wish to establish that the contract between himself and W was void at common law for mistake. If he can establish this, then neither W nor S will have acquired rights under the contract and he will be entitled to assert ownership of the painting. The question is: can he be successful in this contention?

In *Lewis* v *Averay* (1) Lord Denning said that:

> 'When a dealing is had between a seller ... and a person who is actually there present before him, then the presumption in law is that there is a contract, even though there is a fraudulent impersonation by the buyer representing himself as a different man than he is.'

The Court of Appeal derived support from the long-standing decision in *Phillips* v *Brooks Ltd* (2) where the principle was held to be that the fact that one party is mistaken as to the identity of the other does not mean that there is no contract, or that the contract is a nullity and void from the beginning. This principle appears also to have been accepted by the Court of Appeal in *King's Norton Metal Co Ltd* v *Edridge Merret & Co Ltd* (3).

However there are decisions which appear to be contrary to these authorities, and these must be briefly examined. *Ingram* v *Little* (4) is difficult to reconcile with either *Phillips* v *Brooks* or *Lewis* v *Averay*. Although it is a Court of Appeal decision it is submitted that, in view of the criticisms directed against it in *Lewis* and the balance of authority against it, it must be considered of doubtful authority or as turning on its own facts. *Cundy* v *Lindsay* (5), where the contract was found to be void for mistake can be distinguished. The parties there were not *inter praesentes* and the decision can be explained on the ground that the offer was made to one person and accepted by another: this is the explanation given by Lord Denning in the Court of Appeal hearing in *Gallie* v *Lee* (6). The same explanation can be given for the case of *Boulton* v *Jones* (7).

P must be advised therefore that he would be highly unlikely to be able to persuade a court that the contract with W was void for mistake at common law. The equitable remedy of rescission would not avail him for the reason previously given.

The mutual mistake

The actual purchaser of the painting was Q and both he and P were operating under the mistaken belief that the painting was a Goya, whereas it was, in fact, by Picasso. This can be characterised as a mistake as to quality. It appears that this type of mistake rarely makes the contract void at common law. The decision of the House of Lords in *Bell* v *Lever Brothers Ltd* (8) seems to confine operative mistake as to quality to very narrow limits. In *Bell* Lord Atkin said that:

> '... a mistake will not affect assent unless it is the mistake of both parties and is as to the existence of some quality which makes the thing without the quality essentially different from the thing it was believed to be.'

At first sight the mistake here does seem to meet even this restrictive requirement. But, in his speech, Lord Atkin gave a number of examples of mistake as to quality which his Lordship averred would not affect the validity of the contract. One example is the purchase of a picture which both parties believe to be work of an old master, but which turns out to be a modern copy. This is analogous to the situation here. But this example is cogently criticised by Treitel (9). He argues that a mistake of this nature stands on a different level from Lord Atkin's other examples. In *Leaf* v *International Galleries* (10) the purchaser bought a painting under the mistaken belief that it was the work of Constable. There are dicta in that case to the effect that this mistake would not have rendered the contract void. But, as Treitel observes, these dicta are not conclusive; the decision did not turn on that point, the plaintiff only claimed rescission for misrepresentation.

In cases prior to *Bell* the courts, whilst recognising that mistake as to quality *could* make a contract void, have not been ready to do so, see *Kennedy* v *Panama etc Royal Mail Co* (11); *Smith* v *Hughes*(12). In cases since, *Harrison & Jones* v *Bunten & Lancaster*(13) and *F E Rose (London) Ltd* v *W H Pim Jnr & Co Ltd* (14) instance further examples that the courts are not over-ready to find a mistake as to quality to be operative.

In *Nicholson & Venn* v *Smith Marriot* (15) the court would have been prepared to find the contract void for mistake, but the decision did not turn on that point. More recently in *Peco Arts Inc* v *Hazlitt Galleries Ltd* (16) it was a term of the contract that the subject matter was a drawing by a particular artist, but it was, in fact, a copy. The seller conceded that the price was paid 'under a common mistake of fact': however the only issue before the court was whether the claim was statute-barred.

In the latest reported case on this area of the law, *Associated Japanese Bank (International) Ltd* v *Credit du Nord SA* (17), Steyn J conducts a searching examination of the authorities and in particular of the facts of and speeches in *Bell*. It has been suggested, most notably by Lord Denning in *Solle* v *Butcher* (18) and in *Magee* v *Pennine Insurance Co Ltd* (19), that the effect of the decision in *Bell* was to eliminate the possibility of mutual (common) mistake rendering a contract void at common law. Steyn J concludes that such interpretation does not do justice to the speeches in that case, and that such mistake could have this effect, albeit in wholly exceptional circumstances. Steyn J would have been prepared to find that the contract before him was void for mistake as to quality, but again the matter was decided on other grounds.

In view of the uncertainty of the law in this area one cannot with any degree of confidence advise P that he would be successful in a contention that the contract whereby he sold the painting would be found void for mistake.

Nor will equity come to his assistance. It has been established in *Solle* and *Magee* (above) that even where the contract is valid at law equity may be able to provide relief by granting the remedy of rescission; see also *Grist* v *Bailey* (20). However this remedy has been barred, as S, a third party has acquired rights.

Finally an anomaly has to be noted. Q might be able to have the contract with S set aside by the exercise of the equitable jurisdiction. It would seem less than just for him to obtain the remedy denied to P. But perhaps the court would take cognisance of Q's conduct, and on those grounds refuse him equitable relief.

References

1) [1972] 1 QB 198
2) [1919] 2 KB 243

References (continued)

3) (1897) 14 TLR 98
4) [1961] 1 QB 31
5) (1878) 3 App Cas 459
6) [1969] 2 Ch 216
7) (1857) 2 H & N 564
8) [1932] AC 161
9) *The Law of Contract* (7th ed) pp218–19
10) [1950] 2 KB 86
11) (1867) LR 2 QB 580
12) (1871) LR 6 QB 597
13) [1953] 1 QB 646
14) [1953] 2 QB 450
15) (1947) 177 LT 184
16) [1983] 1 WLR 1315
17) [1988] 3 All ER 902
18) [1950] 1 KB 671
19) [1969] 2 QB 507
20) [1967] Ch 532

QUESTION 6

Suggested Solution

An agreement in restraint of trade has been judicially defined as 'one in which a party (the covenantor) agrees with any other party (the covenantee) to restrict his liberty in the future to carry on trade with other persons not parties to the contract in such manner as he chooses' – per Diplock LJ (as he then was) in *Petrofina (Great Britain) Ltd* v *Martin* (1).

It must be conceded that there is a contradiction between the doctrine of restraint of trade and the idea of freedom of contract. The courts are required to balance the competing principles of freedom of contract and freedom of trade. A person is entitled to carry on any lawful trade or occupation that he chooses, but he should also be free to limit that right by a contract into which he freely enters. The doctrine has been justified in different ways. In the earliest cases the restriction on an individual's right to trade was regarded as being 'against the benefit of the Commonwealth' – *Colgate* v *Bachelor* (2). More recently, in *A Schroeder Music Publishing Co Ltd* v *Macaulay* (3) the justification was said, in the House of Lords, to be that it protected the weaker party against the stronger.

The modern law on restraint of trade derives from the House of Lords' decision in *Nordenfelt* v *Maxim Nordenfelt Guns and Ammunition Co Ltd* (4). The policy of the law was formulated by Lord Macnaghten in the following propositions:

a) all restraints of trade, if there is nothing more, are contrary to public policy, and therefore void;

b) but there are exceptions: restraints of trade may be justified by the special circumstances;

c) it is a sufficient justification, indeed it is the only justification, if the restriction is reasonable – reasonable in the interests of the parties and reasonable in the interests of the public.

It is for the party in whose interest the restriction is imposed (the covenantee) to show that it is in the interests of the parties; the onus of showing that it is against the public interest is on the party subject to the restriction (the covenantor).

For the restraint to be reasonable in the interests of the parties, the covenantee must show that he is protecting a legitimate interest, and that the restraint goes no further than is necessary for the protection of that interest. It has been said – and this is an expression of the inherent contradiction – that a restraint cannot be unreasonable if the parties have agreed to it: *NW Salt Co* v *Electrolytic Alkali Co Ltd* (5). But the courts, in their role of custodians of public policy and protectors of the weak against the strong do make these findings.

It is not common for the courts to find that a restraint that is reasonable in the interests of the parties is nevertheless unreasonable in the interests of the public. In *Att Gen for Australia* v *Adelaide Steamship Co* (6) the Privy Council found that they were not aware of any such case. More recently, however, the importance of recognising the public interest has been recognised: *Esso Petroleum Co Ltd* v *Harper's Garage (Stourport) Ltd* (7).

It is necessary to examine various types of contract in which the doctrine operates.

Employment contracts

In such contracts the employee covenants that he will restrict his work and trading activities after the termination of the contract. But the employer is not entitled to protect himself merely from competition: an employee must, as a matter of public policy, be allowed to use the skills and experience he has gained in the employment even if he then competes with his former employer: *Herbert Morris Ltd* v *Saxelby* (8) *Faccenda Chicken Ltd* v *Fowler* (9). The employer must show that he is protecting a legitimate interest; trade secrets or customer connections. Trade secrets consist of the knowledge of some secret process, formula or design. An employer is also entitled to protect his customer connections. But he must show that the employee had a direct, influential relationship with the customers: in this regard the status of the employee will be an important feature; the more senior an employee the more likely it will be that he will have had this kind of relationship.

Having established that there is a legitimate interest to protect, the employer must then satisfy the court that the restraint goes no further that is necessary for the protection of that interest. This involves an examination of the area of the restraint, its duration and the activities which it covers. Much depends on the particular facts. In *Mason* v *Provident Clothing and Supply Co* (10) a restraint which operated within twenty-five miles of London was held to be unreasonable, whereas in *Foster & Sons Ltd* v *Suggett* (11) a restraint operating throughout the United Kingdom was upheld.

In *M & S Drapers* v *Reynolds* (12) a term of five years was held to be unreasonably long; in *Fitch* v *Dewes*(13) a life-long restraint was upheld.

Contracts between the seller and purchaser of a business
In these contracts it is legitimate for the purchaser to protect himself from competition from the former owner of the business. Without such protection the value of the goodwill he has purchased might be rendered nugatory. Whilst similar considerations apply with regard to the reasonableness of the restraint as will be invoked in employment contracts, the courts will subject it to much less scrutiny. The livelihood of the covenantor is not primarily in issue, and the parties will be regarded as being of equal bargaining strength. The courts here will have more regard to the concept of freedom of contract.

Exclusive distributorship agreements
This is a comparatively recent development. The doctrine has been held to apply to an exclusive dealing agreement between a petrol company and a petrol station – a so-called solus agreement – whereby the petrol station undertakes to keep and supply only the company's products. In *Esso Petroleum* v *Harper's Garage* (above) the House of Lords held that the doctrine applies where a person in occupation of land restricts his freedom to trade, it will not apply where a person who had no prior right of occupation acquires land subject to a restriction. This distinction has been adopted in, inter alia, *Cleveland Petroleum Co Ltd* (14).

In *Pharmaceutical Society of Great Britain* v *Dickson* (15) Lord Denning said that the the doctrine of restraint of trade was not confined to particular kinds of contracts. Thus it has been applied to the Football Association's player transfer system – *Eastham* v *Newcastle United FC* (16); to the refusal of the Jockey Club to grant a woman a trainer's licence – *Nagle* v *Fielden* (17); and to a ban on cricketers who joined Mr Kerry Packer's 'circus' – *Greig* v *Insole* (18).

References

1) [1966] Ch 146
2) (1569) Cro Eliz 872
3) [1974] 1 WLR 1308
4) [1894] AC 535
5) [1914[AC 461
6) [1913] AC 781
7) [1968] AC 269
8) [1916] AC 688

References (continued)

9) [1986] ICR 297
10) [1913] AC 724
11) (1918) 35 TLR 87
12) [1957] 1 WLR 9
13) [1921] 2 AC 158
14) [1969] 1 WLR 116
15) [1970] AC 403
16) [1964] Ch 413
17) [1966] 2 QB 633
18) [1978] 1 WLR 302

QUESTION 7

Suggested Solution

This question involves a discussion of the effect of the exclusion clause, and in particular the validity of that exclusion clause under the Unfair Contract Terms Act 1977.

The two purchases made by Cecil, the one for his office and the one for his home, will be discussed in that order.

The purchase for his office

The exclusion clause is clearly incorporated into Cecil's contract with Beta Ltd. He signed the order form containing the clause: *L'Estrange* v *Graucob* (1). This does not require further discussion.

Beta Ltd are in breach of their contract with Cecil. As they have sold the word processor in the course of a business there is the implied condition in the contract under s14(2) Sale of Goods Act 1979 that it is of merchantable quality. As the word processor developed a fault shortly after its purchase there appears to be a clear breach of this implied condition. What must now be considered is whether, as a matter of construction, the clause covers this breach. As a result of the breach Cecil has suffered considerable loss, but it is now settled that there is no breach of contract so 'fundamental' that liability for its breach cannot be excluded as a matter of law: the question is always one of construction: *Suisse Atlantique Societe D'Armament Maritime* v *Rotterdamsche Kolen Centrale* (2); *Photo Production Ltd* v *Securicor Transport Ltd* (3). The clause clearly covers the breach and would, at common law, exclude liability for the consequential loss sustained by Cecil.

The further question remains, however, as to the validity of the clause under the Unfair Contract Terms Act 1977. The Act applies in the present situation by virtue of s1(3)(a) as Beta Ltd's liability for its breach of contract arises 'from things done ... in the course of a business'.

The validity of a clause excluding or restricting liability for breach of a seller's obligations arising from, inter alia, s14(2) Sale of Goods Act 1979 depends on whether or not the purchaser is 'dealing as a consumer'. At first sight, as Cecil has purchased the article for use in his office, s12(1) UCTA would seem definitive that, as he made the contract in the course of a business, he was not dealing as a consumer. However the position is not beyond all doubt in view of the decision of the Court of Appeal in *R & B Customs Brokers Co Ltd* v *United Dominions Trust Ltd* (4). It was held in that case that where a transaction was only incidental to a business activity a degree of regularity was required before the transaction could be said to be an integral part of the business, and so carried on in the course of that business. It is, however, highly likely that the purchase of a word processor, now normal office equipment, would be regarded as an integral part of Cecil's business and not merely incidental to that business. Cecil would not, therefore be considered to be dealing as a consumer.

Under s6(3) of the Act, as against a person dealing otherwise than as a consumer liability for Beta Ltd's breach of contract can only be excluded or restricted in so far as the exclusion clause satisfies the requirement of reasonableness. The question is: does the present clause satisfy this requirement?

The requirement is set out in s11(1) of the Act, which provides that the test is that the clause shall have been a fair and reasonable one 'having regard to the circumstances which were, or ought reasonably to have been, known to or in the contemplation of the parties when the contract was made.' Under s11(5) the burden of proving that the clause is a reasonable one is on Beta Ltd. Section 11(2) provides that, in determining whether the clause is a reasonable one for the purposes of s6(3), regard shall be had to the 'Guidelines' set out in Schedule 2 to the Act. These guidelines refer to such matters as the bargaining strength of the parties, and whether the customer had received an inducement to agree to the clause, or whether, in accepting it, had an opportunity to enter into a similar contract without having to accept a similar term. In *George Mitchell (Chesterhall) Ltd* v *Finney Lock Seeds Ltd* (5) it was indicated that the courts would also take into account the resources of the parties concerned, and the availability of insurance to the party seeking to rely on the clause. Most recently, in *Smith* v *Eric S Bush* (6), Lord Griffiths said that in deciding whether an exclusion clause met the requirement of reasonableness these matters should always be taken into account.

Without all the facts before one it is difficult to give Cecil firm advice as to whether or not the present clause would meet the requirement of reasonableness. There does not appear to be any reason to think that the parties were of unequal bargaining strength. It can also, perhaps, be assumed that Cecil could have entered into a similar contract without having to accept a similar clause. On balance, therefore, it can be tentatively concluded that the clause would be effective, as it would meet the reasonableness requirement. Even if it does not, it is submitted that the cost of hiring extra staff would be regarded as too remote, in accordance with the principles relating to remoteness of damage in contract.

The purchase for Cecil's home
It can be assumed that the clause was also incorporated into this contract.

Under s12(1) Cecil would be regarded as 'dealing as a consumer' if:

a) he neither made the contract in the course of a business nor held himself out as doing so;
b) Beta Ltd did make the contract in the course of a business; and
c) the goods in question were of a type ordinarily sold for private use or consumption.

Clearly (b) is satisfied. It appears that subsection (a) would also be satisfied subject to the reservation that, as Cecil had made the previous purchase for his office, there is the possibility that he might be deemed to have held himself out as having made this contract in the course of a business. With regard to subsection (c) it is submitted that in the present day word processors are ordinarily sold for private use or consumption.

If Cecil is dealing as a consumer in the second contract the exclusion clause is totally ineffective under s6(2) of the Act, and Beta Ltd will be liable to him for the damages he has sustained.

One further point remains to be noted. Under s2(1) of the Act the exclusion or restriction of liability for death or personal injury resulting from negligence is rendered totally ineffective, and Cecil has suffered personal injury. However there is no evidence either way as to negligence on the part of Beta Ltd, so this aspect cannot be further pursued.

References

1) [1934] 2 KB 394
2) [1967] 1 AC 361
3) [1980] AC 827
4) [1988] 1 All ER 847
5) [1983] 2 AC 803
6) [1989] 2 All ER 514

UNIVERSITY OF LONDON
INTERMEDIATE EXAMINATION IN LAWS 1990
for External Students

ELEMENTS OF THE LAW OF CONTRACT

Friday, 15 June : 10.00 am to 1.00 pm

Answer *FOUR* of the following SEVEN questions

1 Alban's house was badly damaged by a storm in March. He engaged Bruno, a builder, to repair the damage. Bruno told Alban that the work would cost £4,000 and that it would be finished by May 1. Alban wanted to put the house up for sale in May and accepted Bruno's terms.

Bruno started work early in April but his progress was hampered by bad weather. Two weeks later he informed Alban that he could only continue with the work if Alban agreed to raise the contract price to £5,000, to cover overtime costs. Reluctantly Alban promised to pay the new price.

Bruno then completed the repairs before the end of April and sent Alban his bill for £5,000, but Alban said that he was now in financial difficulties and could only afford to pay £3,000. Fearing that he would otherwise receive no payment at all, Bruno accepted £3,000 in full settlement.

Bruno recently learned that Alban had plans to go to Africa on safari for two months later this year.

Advise Bruno whether he can recover the rest of the money.

2 Xavier manufactures photocopying machines designed for customers with special requirements. It is his practice not to sell the machines but to lease them to the customers. His standard leasing contract contains the following provisions:

'1 Punctual payment of the agreed monthly rent is deemed to be of the essence of the contract.
2 It is a condition of the contract that the lessee will disconnect the power supply to the machine at the close of business each day.
3 The lessee will notify Xavier immediately of any fault in the machine and will not permit repairs to be carried out by any other person other than Xavier's authorised representative.'

In March 1989 Linus leased a photocopier from Xavier for 3 years on the above terms at a monthly rental of £200. Xavier recently discovered that Linus sometimes allows the power supply to remain connected overnight and has repaired minor faults himself on a few occasions. Linus was also 2 days late in paying last month's rent.

Advise Xavier, who could now charge £300 a month rent if the same photocopier were leased to a new customer.

3 'The remedies for misrepresentation are now just as good as the remedies for breach of contract.'

Discuss.

4 On May 11 A wrote B offering 300 bags of cement at £10 per bag. On May 13 B posted a reply in which he accepted A's offer but added that if he did not hear to the contrary he would assume that the price included delivery to his (B's) yard. The following morning, before B's letter arrived at A's office, A heard a rumour that the price of cement was about to fall and he immediately sent a fax to B stating 'our price of £10 includes delivery'.

On receiving A's fax at 10am on May 14, B wrote and posted a letter to A confirming his acceptance of A's terms. At lunch, however, B also heard the rumour that cement prices were about to fall and at 2pm B sent a fax to A stating 'Decline your offer of cement'.

The price of cement fell to £8 a bag and B refuses to accept any cement from A.

Advise A.

5 'Even if a person has entered into a contract which is unenforceable because of illegality the courts can provide him with redress so long as he comes with clean hands.'

Discuss.

6 In January, in preparation for her daughter Bella's wedding in May, Mrs H agreed to hire J's vintage white Rolls Royce as the bridal car. She engaged K to take the wedding photographs and L to do the catering at the reception.

One week before the wedding J sold the Rolls Royce to M. M is also a photographer, and although he knew about the arrangements made by Mrs H he would not allow the Rolls Royce to be used for Bella's wedding unless he (M) was engaged to take the photographs in place of K.

Mrs H refused to employ M as the photographer and had to hire a modern limousine at a greater cost than the vintage Rolls Royce.

K's flash equipment failed during the service and Bella was heartbroken to find afterwards that there are no pictures of the actual marriage ceremony.

Mrs H, Bella and many more of the guests became ill after eating chicken at the reception which, unknown to L, was contaminated by salmonella.

Advise Mrs H and Bella.

7 Consider the rights and liabilities of Jason, who is 17, in respect of the following transactions:

i) he bought a pair of gold cufflinks costing £200 from Harold, but has not paid for them;

ii) he bought an exercise bicycle from Kenneth and paid for it, but has now decided that exercise is a waste of time and wants to have his money back;

iii) he agreed to work as an assistant in Simon's shop but left after one week because the hours were too long. The contract with Simon provided that it could only be terminated by six months' notice on either side.

QUESTION 1

Suggested Solution

This question involves discussion of two aspects of the doctrine of consideration: *firstly,* whether there was sufficient consideration for Alban's promise to pay the new price; *secondly,* whether the doctrine of promissory estoppel would operate to prevent Bruno recovering the rest of the money.

The suffiency of consideration

The original contract between Alban and Bruno provided for the repair work to be done for the sum of £4,000. Subsequently Alban agreed to the increased price of £5,000, because, it appears, that Bruno would not continue with the work unless he did so. This raises two related issues: was there sufficient consideration for the promise to pay the additional amount? and was that promise exacted by duress?

It is not clear whether the bad weather required Bruno to perform additional work over and above his original contractual obligation. If the completion of the work involved merely the performance of Bruno's existing contractual duty there is authority for the view that this does not constitute sufficient consideration: *Stilk* v *Myrick* (1). This case was declared to be good law in *North Ocean Shipping Co Ltd* v *Hyundai Construction Co Ltd (The Atlantic Baron)* (2). However, the Court of Appeal has purported to refine and limit the principle in *Stilk* v *Myrick* in the recent case of *Williams* v *Roffey Bros & Nicholls (Contractors) Ltd* (3) in which Glidewell LJ expressed the state of the law to be as follows:

> '(i) if A has entered into a contract with B to do work for, or to supply goods or services to, B in return for payment by B and (ii) at some stage before A has completely performed his obligations under the contract B has reason to doubt whether A will, or will be able to, complete his side of the bargain and (iii) B thereupon promises A an additional payment in return for A's promise to perform his contractual obligations on time and (iv) as a result of giving his promise B obtains in practice a benefit, or obviates a disbenefit, and (v) B's promise is not given as a result of economic duress or fraud on the part of A, then (vi) the benefit to B is capable of of being consideration for B's promise, so that the promise will be legally binding.'

It appears from the facts presented that there is the possibility that Alban's promise to pay the additional sum might have been given as a result of enonomic duress on Bruno's part. There is now considerable authority to the effect that a threat to break a contract can constitute economic duress: recent case examples are; *Atlas Express Ltd* v *Kafco (Importers and Distributors) Ltd* (4) and *Vantage Navigation Corporation* v *Suhail & Saud Bahwan Building Materials LCC* (5). In *Pao On* v *Lau Yiu Long* (6) Lord Scarman stated that the relevant factors to be considered in deciding whether a promise had been exacted by duress were: (i) whether the victim had protested; (ii) whether he had an alternative (adequate) legal remedy; (iii) whether he had acted on independent advice; and (iv) whether he had taken timeous steps to avoid the transaction.

Whilst it is not possible to completely rule out the possibility of duress, the mere fact that Alban reluctantly promised to pay the new price does not in itself indicate that there was 'coercion of his will' or that he had 'no real choice' – expressions used in many of the cases to indicate the requisite degree of compulsion. Moreover Alban does not appear to have taken steps to avoid the transaction. It is submitted, therefore, that Alban would not successfully be able to contend that he was acting under duress in promising to pay the new price. Following the decision in *Williams* v *Roffey Bros* (above) it would seem that Alban's promise is legally binding even if Bruno was performing no more than his existing contractual duty. If, by virtue of the delay, Bruno was performing work over and above his previous contractual obligation, he furnished fresh consideration, and Alban would be bound by his promise: *Hartley* v *Ponsonby* (7).

The doctrine of promissory estoppel

It has been argued that Alban is contractually bound to pay the price of £5,000. Even if he is successful in maintaining that the promise to pay the additional amount was exacted by duress, he is clearly obliged to pay the amount of £4,000, as Bruno has performed his obligations under the contract. It appears that Bruno has accepted the lesser sum of £3,000 'in full settlement' At common law the payment of a lesser sum does not discharge the the debtor from payment of the balance unless he has furnished some consideration for the creditor's forebearance. This principle – the rule in *Pinnel's Case* – (8) was affirmed by the House of Lords in *Foakes* v *Beer* (9).

This common law principle has, however, been modified by the development of the doctrine of promissory estoppel. This derives from the decision of the House of Lords in *Hughes* v

Metropolitan Railway Co (10) as developed by Lord Denning MR, notably in *Central London Property Trust Ltd* v *High Trees House Ltd* (11). In delivering the judgment of the Judicial Committee of the Privy Council in *F A Ajayi* v *R T Briscoe (Nigeria) Ltd* (12) Lord Hodson defined the doctrine as follows:

> '... when one party to a contract in the absence of fresh consideration agrees not to enforce his rights an equity will be raised in favour of the other party. This equity is, however, subject to the qualifications (1) that the other party has altered his position, (2) that the promisor can resile from from his promise on giving reasonable notice.which need not be a formal notice, giving the promisee reasonable opportunity of resuming his position, (3) the promise only becomes final and irrevocable if the promisee cannot resume his position.'

The doctrine of promissory estoppel has been criticised as conflicting with the decisions in *Foakes* v *Beer* (above) and *Jorden* v *Money* (13). However, it appears to be firmly established that it can prevail as a defence, though not as a cause of action: *Combe* v *Combe* (14).

The definition of the doctrine can be divided into four elements. (i) There must be a firm and unequivocal promise: *Woodhouse A C Israel Cocoa Ltd S A* v *Nigerian Produce Marketing Co Ltd* (15). This requirement appears to be satisfied. (ii) The promisee must have relied on the promise. The balance of authority is to the effect that it is sufficient if the promisee has altered his position; it is not necessary for him to have done so to his detriment: see per Lord Denning MR in *W J Alan & Co Ltd* v *El Nasr Export and Import Co* (16) and per Robert Goff J in *The Post Chaser* (17). It is not clear to what extent Alban has relied on Bruno's promise, though Lord Denning would hold that merely paying the lesser sum constitutes sufficient reliance: see his judgment in *D & C Builders Ltd* v *Rees* (18). (iii) It must be inequitable for the promisee to go back on his promise. Thus in *D & C Builders* Lord Denning held that the promisor could resile from a promise that had been exacted by intimidation. It may well be, on the given facts, that Alban has dishonestly represented his financial position, and that this would entitle the court to find that it would *not* be inequitable for Bruno to go back on his promise. (iv) The final element is the effect of promissory estoppel; does it extinguish or merely suspend the promisor's rights? In *Tool Metal Manufacturing Co Ltd* v *Tungsten Electric Co Ltd* (19) the Court of Appeal found that as regards existing obligations the effect is extinctive, as regards future obligations it is suspensory. This view has also been expressed extra-judicially by Lord Denning. This would suggest that, if the doctrine operates in Alban's favour, Bruno's rights to the balance have been extinguished.

Lord Hailsham LC stated in *Woodhouse* that the cases based on promissory estoppel 'may need to be reviewed and reduced to a coherent body of doctrine by the courts.' In his Lordship's view 'they do raise problems of coherent exposition which have never been systematically explored.' In view of the uncertainty still prevailing with regard to the doctrine, it would be unwise to give Bruno any positive assurance. On the assumption, however, that Alban has been less than honest regarding his financial position, it is submitted that Bruno can recover the rest of the money.

References

1) (1809) 2 Camp 317
2) [1979] QB 705
3) [1990] 2 WLR 1153
4) [1989] 1 All ER 641
5) [1989] 1 LLoyd's Rep 138
6) [1980] AC 614
7) (1857) 7 El & Bl 872
8) (1602) 5 Co Rep 117a
9) (1884) 9 App Cas 605
10) (1877) 2 App Cas 439
11) [1947] 1 KB 130
12) [1964] 1 WLR 1326
13) (1854) 5 HLC 185
14) [1951] 2 KB 215
15) [1972] AC 74
16) [1972] 2 QB 189
17) [1982] 1 All ER 19
18) [1966] 2 QB 617
19) [1955] 1 WLR 761

QUESTION 2

Suggested Solution

The issue raised by this question is the relative importance of contractual terms. Traditionally the terms of a contract were classified as conditions or warranties. A condition has been defined as an 'essential term' of the contract; or one where 'performance of the stipulation (went) to the very root ... of the contract': *Bentsen* v *Taylor* (1). A breach of condition can be regarded by the injured party as a repudiation of the contract and entitles him to terminate it and thereby discharge himself from further obligations. A warranty is a less important term, its breach does not entitle the injured party to terminate the contract, but confines him to a remedy in damages. Warranty is defined in the Sale of Goods Act 1979 in s61(1) as a term 'collateral to the main purpose of (the) contract, the breach of which gives rise to a claim for damages, but not a right to reject the goods and treat the contract as repudiated.'

A further category has, however, been recognised. Certain terms cannot be classified as conditions or warranties, but whether they are to be treated as conditions or waranties depends on the nature of the breach. Such terms are called 'innonimate terms'. This approach was adopted in the earlier cases of *Bettini* v *Gye* (2) and *Poussard* v *Spiers* (3). A further example is the case of *Aerial Advertising Co* v *Batchelor's Peas Ltd* (4). But the concept of the innonimate term was first expressly recognised by the Court of Appeal decision in *Hong Kong Fir Shipping Co Ltd* v *Kawasaki Kishen Kaisha Ltd* (5). In the course of his judgment Diplock LJ (as he then was) said that many contractual undertakings could not be classified as conditions or warranties.

> 'Of such undertakings all that can be predicated is that some breaches will and others will not give rise to an event which will deprive the party not in default of substantially the whole benefit which it was intended that he should obtain from the contract ... .'

In *Bunge Corporation, New York* v *Tradax Export SA, Panama* (6) Lord Scarman said that:

> 'Unless the contract makes it clear, either by express provision or by necessary implication arising from its nature, purpose and circumstances ... that a particular stipulation is a condition or only a

warranty, it is an innonimate term the remedy for a breach of which depends on the nature, consequences and effect of the breach.'

A contractual term is then a condition if the parties expressly intended it to be so, or if it is classified as such by statute, or judicial decision; otherwise whether it is treated as a condition or merely as a warranty depends on the nature extent and consequences of the breach.

In the present problem Xavier wishes to terminate the contract. Linus has clearly been in breach of the provisions set out. The question is: are any of these breaches to be regarded as a breach of condition? Each of the provisions must be considered in turn.

The provision for punctual payment

It is provided that this 'is deemed to be of the essence of the contract.' The actual breach of this provision is trivial – Linus was two days late in paying last month's rent – but if the term is a condition any breach, however trivial, would justify Xavier in treating it as a repudiatory breach, and entitle him to terminate the contract.

Time is often of the essence in commercial contracts – see, for example, *The Mihalis Angelos* (7). But a failure to make a punctual payment would not necessarily be considered to be repudiatory in a contract such as the present one: *Financings Ltd* v *Baldock* (8). Clearly the nature of the breach here is not one that could be regarded as depriving Xavier of the substantial benefit of the contract. However, in *Lombard North Central plc* v *Butterworth* (9) where there was a similar clause, the Court of Appeal held that even though the failure to pay promptly was not repudiatory, the clause had the effect of making failure to pay on time a breach of condition. In view of that decision, whilst it is harsh, it seems inescapable that Xavier would be able to rely on the breach by Linus as constituting a breach of condition, and thus entitling him to terminate the contract.

The provision with regard to disconnecting the power supply

This clause is described as a 'condition'. This is not conclusive; the court would have to be satisfied that the parties intended to use the word in the technical sense. In *Schuler A G* v *Wickman Machine Tool Sales Ltd* (10) one particular clause was called a condition and no other term in the 20 clauses was described as a condition. It was argued that because that particular clause was described as a condition any breach of it by the one party entitled the other party to terminate the contract. This argument was rejected by the House of Lords. Lord Reid held that the use of the word 'condition' was perhaps a strong indication that the parties intended the clause to be a condition in the technical sense, but it was not conclusive evidence. Their Lordships were able to come to the conclusion that the technical use of the word was not intended by a consideration of the contract as a whole. A further clause in the contract provided for notice to be given of a 'material breach'. This enabled the House of Lords to interpret the word in a non-technical sense. Lord Reid did say, however, that, but for this further clause, he would have found difficulty in reaching this conclusion.

The question here is not without difficulty. It seems unreasonable for Xavier to be held entitled to terminate the contract because of one failure by Linus to disconnect the power supply. But this would follow if this provision is interpreted as a condition, and it is so described. There is not the escape from that conclusion by a clause similar to the one in *Schuler*. There does not appear to be any provision for notice to Linus requiring him to remedy or desist from the breach. Accordingly it is submitted that this provision too would be regarded by the court as a condition, the breach of which would entitle Xavier to terminate.

The provision regarding faults and repairs

This provision appears to be one which cannot be categorised as being a condition or a warranty. It is typically a clause which would require consideration of – in Lord Scarman's words – 'the nature effect and consequences of the breach'. It is therefore an innominate term. The breaches of this provision that have occurred are not of sufficient gravity to justify treating them as breaches of condition. Xavier would not be able to rely on them to justify termination.

In conclusion it is submitted that although Xavier cannot rely on the third provision as entitling him to terminate he can do so by virtue of the breaches of the the first two provisions. It must be admitted that this conclusion could be regarded as over-technical, but the authorities do not appear to allow for any alternative.

References

1) [1893] 2 QB 274
2) (1876) 1 QBD 183
3) (1876) 1 QBD 351
4) [1938] 2 All ER 788
5) [1962] 2 QB 26
6) [1980] 1 Lloyd's Rep 294
7) [1971] 1 QB 164
8) [1963] 2 QB 104
9) [1987] QB 527
10) [1974] AC 235

QUESTION 3

Suggested Solution

This question self-evidently requires a discussion of the remedies for misrepresentation and the remedies for breach of contract. However, it is not sufficient merely to set out the respective remedies; an evaluation of the remedies and a comparison of their utilities must be made.

The question can usefully be answered by firstly setting out the remedies for breach of contract and then examining those for misrepresentation in order to discuss the given quotation.

Breach of contract

The basic common law remedy for breach of contract is an award of damages. The plaintiff is only entitled to terminate the contract – Treitel and Atiyah employ the expression 'rescission for breach' – where the breach is one of condition. The purpose of an award of damages is to compensate the plaintiff for the loss he has sustained. The types of loss for which damages can be recovered are: (i) loss of bargain; (ii) reliance loss; and (iii) restitution.

Loss of bargain

The purpose of an award of damages for loss of bargain is to put the plaintiff 'so far as money can do it ... in the same situation as if the contract had been performed'; *Robinson* v *Harman* (1). This is subject to the overriding limitation that the damages are not too remote. The leading cases in this context are: *Hadley* v *Baxendale* (2); *Victoria Laundry (Windsor) Ltd* v *Newman Industries Ltd* (3); and *The Heron II* (4). The principle derived from these cases is that the plaintiff is entitled to be compensated for such loss as was reasonably within the contemplation of the parties.

Reliance loss

As an alternative to loss of bargain the plaintiff is entitled to be compensated for the wasted expenditure he has incurred in the performance of the contract. The purpose here being to put the plaintiff in the position he would have been in if the contract had never been made: see *Anglia Television Ltd* v *Reed* (5). Again this is subject to the principle regarding remoteness of damage.

Restitution

Under this heading the defendant may be compelled to restore to the plaintiff the benefit he has received under the contract.

(The equitable remedies for breach of contract are an order for specific performance and an injunction, but discussion of these remedies is beyond the scope of this question.)

Misrepresentation

The remedies for misrepresentation are rescission and, in certain circumstances, damages.

Rescission

Rescission is an equitable remedy, which involves restoring the parties to the position they were in before the contract was concluded. It is available for all types of misrepresentation, whether fraudulent, negligent or innocent – these latter two are defined below.

Misrepresentation renders a contract voidable. The plaintiff can elect to affirm or rescind the contract. This remedy is often a satisfactory one for the plaintiff, it is indeed a drastic remedy. However, there are certain bars to the right to rescind. The right can be lost: (i) by affirmation of the contract by the plaintiff – *Long* v *Lloyd* (6); (ii) where restitutio in integrum is not possible – *Clarke* v *Dickson* (7); (iii) by the intervention of third party rights – *Phillips* v *Brooks Ltd* (8); and (iv) by the lapse of time – *Leaf* v *International Galleries* (9).

As has been seen the right to rescind for breach of contract only obtains where there has been a breach of condition. Before the Misrepresentation Act 1967 it was doubtful if the right to rescind for misrepresentation survived if the misrepresentation had become a term of the contract. Section 1(a) of the Act provides, however, that a person is entitled to rescind notwithstanding that the misrepresentation has become a term of the contract, if he would otherwise be entitled to rescind without alleging fraud. In some sense, therefore, rescission for misrepresentation is a more powerful remedy.

Because rescission may prove to be a drastic remedy the court is given a discretion under s2(2) of the Act, other than where the misrepresentation is fraudulent, to declare the contract subsisting and award damages in lieu of rescission if of the opinion that it would be equitable to do so.

Damages

The entitlement to damages depends on the nature of the misrepresentation. Damages in the tort of deceit are available for fraudulent misrepresentation. The defendant may be held liable for all the loss flowing from the fraudulent misrepresentation even if this could not have been foreseen: *Doyle* v *Olby (Ironmongers) Ltd* (10). Aggravated damages may be recoverable *Archer* v *Brown* (11).

Prior to the Misrepresentation Act where a misrepresentation was not fraudulent it was regarded as innocent, and for an innocent misrepresentation damages were not available. All that could be granted was the award of an indemnity, reimbursing the plaintiff for the expenses the contract itself had required him to incur: *Whittington* v *Seale-Hayne* (12). This often posed a difficulty for the plaintiff. Unless he could prove fraud his only remedy would be rescission, and this right he might have lost through no fault of his own – for example by the intervention of third party rights. Moreover fraud is difficult to prove, see the stringent requirements set out by Lord Herschell in *Derry* v *Peek* (13).

This situation was altered by the Misrepresentation Act. Under s2(1) where a person has entered into a contract after a misrepresentation has been made to him, and has suffered loss as a result, and the person making the misrepresentation would have have been liable in damages if the misrepresentation had been fraudulent, he will still be liable even though it was not fraudulent, unless he proves that he had reasonable ground to believe and did believe up to the time the contract was made, that the facts represented were true. Thus, in comparison with an allegation of fraud, the onus of proof is reversed. Where the defendant is not able to discharge this onus, his misrepresentation is termed, for convenience, negligent misrepresentation, and this may incur liability in damages.

Some doubt was caused as to the measure of damages under s2(1). There are authorities suggesting that the contractual measure applies, which would compensate the plaintiff for his loss of bargain. However the more generally held view is that damages are to be assessed on the tortious basis, the purpose of which is to put the plaintiff in the position he would have been in if the wrong had not bee committed: *Andre & Cie SA* v *Ets Michel Blanc & Fils* (14); *Sharneyford Supplies Ltd* v *Edge* (15).

Parallel with this statutory innovation the House of Lords developed liability at common law for the tort of negligent misstatement in *Hedley Byrne & Co* v *Heller & Partners* (16). Liabilty here, however, depends on there being a 'special relationship' between the parties, which is not required under s2(1).

In the absence of the *Hedley Byrne* situation, where the defendant discharges the onus imposed on him by s2(1), the misrepresentation is innocent and he will not incur liability in damages, but only for the payment of an indemnity.

It remains to say that where the court exercise its discretion under s2(2), and awards damages in lieu of rescission, the measure of damages is not clear. It is suggested that the award may well constitute an amount to compensate the plaintiff for the loss of his right to rescind.

In conclusion the remedies for misrepresentation may not be as good as the remedies for breach of contract where the right to rescind has been lost, where the representation is innocent and with regard to the measure of damages.

References

1) (1848) 1 Ex 850
2) (1854) 9 Ex 341
3) [1949] 2 KB 528
4) [1969] 1 AC 350
5) [1972] 1 QB 60
6) [1958] 1 WLR 753
7) (1858) 120 ER 463
8) [1919] 2 KB 243
9) [1950] 2 KB 86
10) [1969] 2 QB 158
11) [1985] QB 401
12) (1900) 82 LT 49
13) (1889) 14 App Cas 337
14) [1977] 2 Lloyd's Rep 166
15) [1987] 2 WLR 367
16) [1964] AC 465

QUESTION 4

Suggested Solution

This is a question which requires discussion of some of the common problems of offer and acceptance. As with most questions in this area it is necessary to analyse each stage of the transaction chronologically.

The letter from A to B of May 11 is clearly an offer. What has first to be considered is whether B's reply of May 13 is an acceptance or a counter-offer. Treitel defines an acceptance as 'a final and unqualified expression of assent to the terms of an offer.' (1). If a new term is introduced in the reply it is not an acceptance, but a counter-offer. But if B does not intend to introduce a new term in his reply the statement with regard to delivery does not prevent it being an acceptance: *Butler Machine Tool Co Ltd* v *Ex-cell-o Corporation (England) Ltd* (2). It is at least possible that delivery to B's yard is not a new term, but one that the law would imply, if that was the custom in the particular trade. In that event, as A made the offer through the post the postal rule would apply and there would have been an acceptance of A's offer when B posted his letter: *Adams* v *Lindsell* (3); *Henthorn* v *Fraser* (4). However this is unlikely as B contemplates a reply to the contrary.

Having ruled out the possibility that B's letter is an acceptance, it follows that it is a counter-offer. It has been long-established that a counter-offer destroys the original offer and constitutes a fresh offer which the original offeror, now the offeree, is free to accept or reject: *Hyde* v *Wrench* (5). B is now the offeror in his letter of May 13 and he states that he assumes that the price includes delivery unless he hears to the contrary. An offeror cannot impose silence on the offeree:*Felthouse* v *Bindley* (6). But, as Treitel suggests (7) this rule is arguably for the protection of the offeree, the offeror can waive communication of acceptance and be contractually bound by the offeree's silence. Thus the further possibility must be considered that, there being no reply to the contrary, a contract is concluded on the terms of B's letter. However this proposition is not free from doubt, and it is necessary to proceed to the next stage of negotiations.

If no contract has as yet been concluded at this stage A's fax stating that 'our price of £10 includes delivery' constitutes a fresh offer. When he sends this fax A has not received B's letter, and there is authority for the view that cross offers are not an acceptance of each other: *Tinn* v *Hoffman & Co* (8). It is assumed, therefore that, at this stage, a contract has still not been concluded.

If that assumption is correct then A's fax is a further fresh offer. B writes to the effect that he accepts that offer. The next question is – has that acceptance been effectively communicated?

As stated above the normal postal rule is that acceptance is deemed to be communicated when the letter of acceptance is posted. However it is questionable whether the postal rule applies to an offer made through the medium of a fax. It is, of course, clear that an offeree must comply with the offeror's stipulated mode of acceptance but he may adopt a mode as or more expeditious than the one prescribed: *Manchester Diocesan Council for Education* v *Commercial and General Investments Ltd* (9). However the transmission of the offer by fax implies that A requires instantaneous communication, and that a posted acceptance would be ineffective. In *Quenerduaine* v *Cole* (10) it was held that it would not normally be reasonable to attempt to accept a telegraphic offer by posting a letter. *A fortiori* it would not be reasonable to answer a fax message by letter. A strict application of this principle would lead to the conclusion that as B's letter of acceptance is invalid no contract has been concluded.

This conclusion, however, would violate common sense. B has elected to use the post and should not be allowed to avail himself of the argument that the method he has himself chosen is ineffective. In *Holwell Securities Ltd* v *Hughes* (11) Lawton LJ said that the postal rule probably does not operate 'where its application would produce manifest inconvenience and absurdity.' It is submitted that his Lordship's approach should be adapted, and that here *not* to apply the postal rule would lead similarly to 'inconvenience and absurdity'. It must be concluded, therefore, that the offer made by A through the medium of the fax has been effectively accepted by B.

B has, however, purports to revoke his acceptance by the fax which he in turn transmits. There is no clear authority in English law as to whether an offeree, who has posted a letter of acceptance, can revoke his acceptance by a speedier method of communication. A strict application of the postal rule would deny that this is possible. This view derives support from the The New Zealand decision in *Wenckheim* v *Arndt* (12) and that of a South African court in *A to Z Bazaars (Pty) Ltd* v *Minister of Agriculture* (13). There is a US decision to the contrary: *Dick* v *US* (14).

In the absence of binding authority it is submitted that, as a matter of policy, B should not be permitted to withdraw his acceptance, especially in view of B's clear prior indication that he wished to accept A's offer provided that the price included delivery. A should therefore be advised that B is contractually bound to accept delivery of the 300 bags of cement.

This conclusion has been arrived at by applying the traditional analysis of offer and acceptance. An alternative approach should be considered. In *Butler Machine Tool Co* (above) Lord Denning MR had the view that in many cases 'our traditional analysis of offer, counter-offer, rejection, acceptance and so forth is out- of- date.' Lord Denning said that this had been observed by Lord Wilberforce in *New Zealand Shipping Co Ltd* v *A M Satterthwaite & Co Ltd (The Eurymedon)* (15). He went on to say that:

> 'The better way is to look at all the documents passing between the parties and glean from them, or from the conduct of the parties, whether they have reached agreement on all material points ... '.

Lord Denning also rejected the conventional analysis in favour in of this approach in *Gibson* v *Manchester City Council* (16). But this did find favour in the House of Lords, where Lord Diplock said that by departing from the conventional approach the majority of the Court of Appeal had been led into error. In the course of his speech Lord Diplock said:

> ' ... there may be certain types of contract, though I think they are exceptional, which do not fit easily into the normal analysis of a contract as being constituted by offer and acceptance; but a contract alleged to have been made by an exchange of correspondence between the parties in which the successive communications other than the first are in reply to one another is not one of these.'

In the present question the application of Lord Denning's approach would also lead to the conclusion that a binding contract existed between the parties; they had, it is submitted, clearly 'come to an agreement on everything that was material'.

In view of Lord Diplock's strictures, however, a court might well be chary of adopting such an approach. Nor would it be necessary to do so: the conventional approach leads to the same result.

References

1) The Law of Contract (7th ed) p13
2) [1979] 1 WLR 401
3) (1818) 1 B & Ald 681

References (continued)

4) [1892] 2 Ch 27
5) (1840) 3 Beav 334
6) (1862) 11 CB(NS) 869
7) op cit pp27–28
8) (1873) 29 LT 271
9) [1970] 1WLR 241
10) (1883) 32 WR 185
11) [1974] 1 WLR 155
12) (NZ) 1 JR 73 (1873)
13) (1974) (4) SA 392(C)
14) 82 F Supp 326 (1949)
15) [1975] AC 154
16) [1979] 1 WLR 294

QUESTION 5

Suggested Solution

This question requires discussion of the circumstances in which a party to an illegal contract, although he cannot enforce the contract, may be able to recover money or property passing under it.

The general rule is expressed in the maxim *in pari delicto potior est conditio possidentis*. This means that where the parties are equally culpable with regard to the illegality, recovery of money or property is not permitted, with the consequence that the person in possession is in the stronger position. However, there are exceptions to the rule. The broad principle behind the exceptions is that a court will decide whether or not to permit recovery depending on which option would give better effect to the prohibition of the contract.

The exceptions can be grouped under four headings: (i) where the parties are not in pari delicto; (ii) the contract has been entered into under a mistake; (iii) the person seeking recovery has repudiated the illegal contract; and (iv) where the plaintiff does not rely on the illegal contract to claim recovery. These will be considered in turn.

The parties not in pari delicto

Where a statute has been enacted for the protection of a particular class of persons it is in the interests of public policy that a plaintiff within that class should be permitted recovery. Thus in *Kiriri Cotton Co Ltd* v *Dewani* (1) where the prohibition was against the payment of premiums exacted by landlords for the granting of a lease the tenant was allowed to recover the premium he had paid: see also *Kasumu* v *Baba-Egbe* (2).

If a plaintiff has been coerced into entering into an illegal contract by duress recovery may be allowed: *Smith* v *Cuff* (3).

Recovery will also be possible where the plaintiff enters into an illegal contract, being induced to do so by a fraudulent misrepresentation which concealed the illegality: *Hughes* v *Liverpool Victoria Legal Friendly Society* (4).

The contract entered into under a mistake

Where a party enters into an illegal contract under a mistake of fact he may not be without a remedy where he is innocent of the facts which render the contract illegal. Indeed the innocent party may in some circumstance be able to enforce the contract. Whether he is able to do so depends on the nature of the prohibition. If the statute prohibits both parties from concluding the contract neither the innocent nor the guilty party may enforce it: *Re Mahmoud and Ispahani* (5). Where the prohibition is directed against one party, coupled with a sanction, the innocent party may be permitted to enforce the contract, depending on public policy considerations: *Archbolds (Freightage) Ltd* v *S Spanglett Ltd* (6). *Phoenix General Insurance of Greece* v *Adas* (7).

Even if the innocent party is not able to enforce the contract, which he entered into under a mistake of fact, he may be able to recover money or property: *Oom* v *Bruce* (8). There can be no recovery where the mistake is one of law: *Harse* v *Pearl Assurance Co* (9).

Repudiation of the illegal contract

It is in the interests of public policy that people should be encouraged to repudiate illegal contracts into which they may have entered. A party is therefore afforded a *locus poenitentiae* and may withdraw from the illegal contract and recover his payment. But the repudiation must be in time. In *Kearley* v *Thomson* (10) recovery of a payment was not allowed because the illegal purpose had been substantially carried out when the plaintiff sought to withdraw from the transaction. In contrast, where there was an illegal scheme to defraud creditors, the plaintiff had repudiated the scheme before the purpose had been carried out, and was permitted to recover the payment *Taylor* v *Bowers* (11).

Furthermore the repudiation must be voluntary. It will not avail a plaintiff if his repudiation of the illegal contract is occasioned by a third party or by the other party's breach of that contract: *Bigos* v *Bousted* (12). A plaintiff cannot be said to have come with clean hands if the repudiation has been forced on him by external pressures.

No reliance on the illegal contract

A plaintiff may be able to recover property (but not generally money) if he can establish a right to that property independent of the illegal contract. In Bowmakers Ltd v Barnet Instruments Ltd (13) the plaintiffs delivered ceratin machine tools to the defendants under illegal hire-purchase agreements. The defendants, in breach of the agreements, failed to pay the due instalments, sold some of the machine tools and refused to return the remainder. The defendants, by virtue of their breaches of contract, no longer had any right to possess the goods. The plaintiffs were successful in an action for damages for the tort of conversion: they were able to establish their right to the goods without relying on the illegal transactions. See also *Belvoir Finance Co* v *Stapleton* (14).

Recovery will not be permitted under this heading where the plaintiff is compelled to plead the illegality in order to found his claim: see *Taylor* v *Chester* (15).

References

1) [1960] AC 192
2) [1956] AC 539
3) (1817) 6 M & S 160
4) [1916] 2 KB 482
5) [1921] 2 KB 716
6) [1961] 1 QB 374
7) [1987] 2 All ER 155
8) (1810) 12 East 225
9) [1904] 1 KB 558
10) (1890) 24 QBD 742
11) (1876) 1 QBD 291
12) [1951] 1 All ER 92
13) [1945] KB 65
14) [1970] 3 WLR 530
15) (1869) LR 4 QB 309

QUESTION 6

Suggested Solution

The main issues raised here are those arising out of the doctrine of privity of contract. The question also requires some discussion of the availability of damages for distress for breach of contract.

The basic rule of privity was expressed in the following terms by Viscount Haldane in *Dunlop Pneumatic Tyre Co Ltd* v *Selfridge & Co Ltd* (1):

> ' ... in the law of England certain principles are fundamental. One is that only a person who is a party to a contract can sue on it. Our law knows nothing of a jus quaesitum tertio arising by way of contract.'

The consequence of the doctrine of privity of contract is that a third party cannot acquires benefits under a contract to which he was not a party, nor can a third party have obligations imposed on him by such contract. The doctrine has been characterised as 'a blot on our law and most unjust' by Dillon J in *Forster* v *Golf and Equestrian Centre* (2). Lord Scarman appeared to call for its abolition in *Woodar Investment Development Ltd* v *Wimpey Construction (UK) Ltd* (3). As long ago as 1937 the Law Revision Committee (4) recommended that where a a contract expressly conferred a benefit on a third party it should be directly enforceable by the third party. However, these reforms have not as yet been implemented, though there are statutory exceptions to the privity rule and it may be possible to circumvent it.

Adverting to the particular problem, it is necessary to examine each of the contracts in turn.

The contract with J for the hire of the Rolls Royce

J is clearly in breach of contract by selling the car to M. Mrs H can sustain an action against him for the breach. The remedy of specific performance is not, of course, available as performance is impossible *Watts* v *Spence* (5). Her remedy against J is a claim for damages. In accordance with the general principle that the purpose of an award of damages is to put her in the position she would have been in if the contracted had been performed, she would be entitled to the difference between the contract price and and the price she has to pay for the other vehicle. It is possible that the she might have suffered distress at not being able to obtain the vintage Rolls Royce. The question of damages for distress is dealt with below.

M, to whom the Rolls Royce has been sold, knows of Mrs H's contractual rights, but refuses to allow her to exercise them unless he is engaged as the photographer. Because of the rules of privity of contract, this does not afford Mrs H any contractual claim against M: *Dunlop* v *Selfridge* (above). M is not a party to the contract between Mrs H and J and the obligations of that contract cannot be imposed on him at common law. Nor would equity impose any liability on him. The rule in *Tulk* v *Moxhay* (6) appears to be confined to interests in land: the purported extension of that rule by the Judicial Committee of the Privy Council in *Lord Strathcona Steamship Co* v *Dominion Coal Co* (7) has never been followed in the English courts and that decision must be regarded as doubtful authority; see the judgments of Diplock J in *Port Line Ltd* v *Ben Line Steamers Ltd* (8) and Denning LJ in *Bendall* v *McWhirter* (9).

The one possibility of circumventing the privity rule and fixing M with liability is in the law of Tort which recognises liability for interfering with contractual rights: *Lumley* v *Gye* (10); *British Motor Trade Association* v *Salvadori* (11). (There are a number of trade union cases in this area of the law, but citation of them is beyond the scope of this question). It is an essential ingredient of the tort that the wrongdoer knew of the contractual rights, but M possessed that knowledge and could not, it appears, escape liability.

The contract with K for the wedding photographs

It is assumed that the failure to take the photographs constitutes a breach of contract on K's part. Section 13 Supply of Goods and Services Act 1982 imposes a duty on the supplier of a service to carry out that service with reasonable skill and care. The question is: to whom, and to what extent, is he liable for that breach?

The question suggests that it is Bella, and not Mrs H, who has suffered distress as a result of the breach. Two points emerge for discussion; one, the extent to which a court will award damages for distress; two, who can sue for such distress.

Damages for distress have been awarded in cases involving contracts for a holiday: *Jackson* v *Horizon Holidays Ltd* (12); *Jarvis* v *Swan's Tours Ltd* (13). But an award of damages for distress is limited to certain classes of cases. In *Bliss* v *South East Thames Regional Health Authority*(14) Dillon LJ held that such an award should be confined to cases 'where the contract which has been broken was itself a contract to provide peace of mind or freedom from distress.' In *Hayes and Another* v *James & Charles Dodd* (15) Staughton LJ was of the opinion that the class might be somewhat wider than that 'But it should not include any case where the object of the contract was not comfort or pleasure or the relief of discomfort, but simply carrying on a commercial activity with a view to profit.'

A claim for damages for distress would, it is submitted, fall at least within the limits set by Staughton LJ. (By the same token Mrs H might well have a claim for damages for distress against J for his failure to supply the Rolls Royce).

The question of who can sustain a claim for the distress against K must next be addressed. The privity rule is the clear difficulty in the way of an action by Bella. The rule that a benefit cannot be conferred on a third party was established in *Tweddle* v *Atkinson* (16) and affirmed by the House of Lords in *Beswick* v *Beswick* (17). There is no evidence on the facts presented to indicate that Mrs H acted as Bella's agent, or that Bella was in any sense a party to the contract.

Nor can Mrs H sue for Bella's loss. In *Jackson* v *Horizon Holidays* Lord Denning held that the promisee could always sue for the third party's loss, but this view was expressly disapproved by the House of Lords in *Woodar* v *Wimpey*. It must be concluded, therefore, that no claim will lie against K.

The contract with L for the catering

The question suggests that there has been no negligence on L's part, so no action in tort will lie. So far as as a contractual claim is concerned L appears to be in breach of the implied term in s14(2) Sale of Goods Act 1979 in that he has failed to supply goods of a merchantable quality. Clearly Mrs H, as a party to the contract, can sue for damages for the illness she has suffered. What of Bella's illness? In *Woodar* v *Wimpey* Lord Wilberforce 'explained' the decision in *Jackson* v *Horizon Holidays*. Although he rejected the view that the promisee can sue for the third party's loss, he was not prepared to part from the actual decision in that case. He said that it could be supported as a special type of contract, examples of which are persons contracting for family holidays or ordering meals in a restaurant, calling for special treatment – all the members of the family would be regarded as parties to the contract. Lord Russell appeared to hold that he did not criticise the outcome in *Jackson* because there the third party's loss was also the promisee's loss.

The strict application of the privity rule would debar Bella from a claim against L, and would also prevent Mrs H from suing for Bella's loss. However, the decision in *Jackson*, as justified by the House of Lords in *Wimpey*, permits the possibility that Bella can sustain an action on the basis that she too was a party to the contract with L, or that Mrs H can claim that Bella's loss was also her own. Whether this can be extended to the guests is extremely doubtful.

References

1) [1915] AC 847
2) (1981) 125 Sol Jo 397
3) [1980] 1 WLR 277
4) 6th Interim Report (Cmd 5449)
5) [1976] Ch 165
6) (1848) 2 Ph 774
7) [1926] AC 108
8) [1958] 2 QB 146
9) [1952] 2 QB 466
10) (1853) 2 E & B 216
11) [1949] Ch 556
12) [1975] 1 WLR 1468
13) [1973] 1 QB 233
14) [1987] ICR 700
15) (1988) The Times 14 July
16) (1861) 1 B & S 393
17) [1968] AC 58

QUESTION 7

Suggested Solution

Jason, being under the age of 18, is a minor in law – s1 Family Law Reform Act 1969. This question, therefore, raises the issue of the contractual capacity of minors. Jason has entered into three contracts: (i) the purchase of the cufflinks from Harold; (ii) the purchase of the exercise bicycle from Kenneth; and (iii) the agreement to work as an assistant in Simon's shop. These three transactions will be considered in turn.

The purchase of the cufflinks

A minor is bound by a contract for necessary goods – described in *Peters* v *Fleming* (1) as 'such goods as are fit to maintain the particular person in the state, station and degree ... in which he is.' Section 3(3) Sale of Goods Act 1979 defines 'necessaries' as 'goods suitable to the condition in life of the minor ... and to his actual requirements at the time of the sale and delivery.'

There is a paucity of modern authority as to the nature of necessaries. In *Peters* v *Fleming* jewellery supplied to the son of a wealthy man were found to be necessaries, but in *Ryder* v *Wombwell* (2) the court set aside the verdict of a jury that similar items were necessaries. It is, perhaps, doubtful whether these two mid-nineteenth cases can provide much guidance in the present day.

The onus is on Harold to show that the cufflinks were necessaries. He would have to prove not only that they were capable of being necessaries, but that they actually were necessaries in Jason's case: *Nash* v *Inman* (3). It seems unlikely that Harold could discahrge this onus – it is difficult to conceive that gold cufflinks costing £200 could be regarded as necessaries for a 17 year old.

If they are not necessaries the contract is unenforceable against Jason. The purchase price cannot be recovered from him. However, Harold is not without a remedy. Equity provides the remedy of restitution where non-necessary goods were sold and transferred to a minor who was guilty of fraud. At common law restitution can also be ordered in certain cases of quasi-contract. This remedy is now also afforded by statute: s3(1) Minors' Contracts Act 1987 gives the court a discretion to order the minor to transfer to the plaintiff any property acquired by the minor under a contract which was not enforceable against him. There does not appear to be any reason why the court should not exercise its discretion in favour of Harold and order Jason to restore the cufflinks to him.

The possibility should briefly be considered that, by virtue of Jason's particular circumstances, these articles are considered to be necessaries, although – as has been indicated – this is thought to be unlikely. If they are necessaries s3(2) Sale of Goods Act provides that the minor must pay a reasonable price for them.This may not be the contract price, but there is insufficient information to determine what it might be.

The purchase of the exercise bicycle from Kenneth

The question here again is whether this article can be considered to be a necessary. A helpful authority is, possibly, *Clyde Cycle Co* v *Hargreaves* (4), which concerned the purchase of a racing bicycle by an apprentice. This was held to be a necessary. However, too much reliance should not be placed on that case. It is not conclusive with regard to the present problem; much depends on the price of the exercise bicycle and on Jason's particular requirements.

It is necessary to consider both possibilties; that the bicycle is not a necessary and that it is.

If it is not a necessary the contract would not be enforceable against Jason. But it appears that he has already paid for it. He cannot recover the money paid simply on the ground that he was not bound by the contract because of his minority. Treitel (5) cites three authorities in support of this proposition: *Wilson* v *Kearse* (6): *Corpe* v *Overston* (7); and *Ex p Taylor* (8). The right to reject the goods and reclaim the purchase price would have to be based on grounds that were also available to an adult.

If the bicycle is a necessary then Jason is bound by the contract, subject to the aforestated provision in the Sale of Goods Act that he would have been required to pay only 'a reasonable price', not necessarily the contract price. But what a reasonable price might have been is of academic interest: he has made the payment and, as indicated by the above three authorities, once the minor has performed the contract, he cannot recover the money.

The contract to work for Simon

This is a a contract of service, and the rule in this regard is that a minor is bound by beneficial contracts of service. The test is this: if the contract is to the minor's benefit as a whole, he will be bound by it, nothwithstanding that it contains certain provisions that are to his disadvantage: *Clements* v *L & N W Ry* (9); *Doyle* v *White City Stadium Ltd* (10): he will not be bound by a service contract if it is on the whole harsh and oppressive: *De Francesco* v *Barnum* (11).

It is difficult to be certain whether or not Jason's contract with Simon would fall into the latter category. No information is given as to the hours of work, the other conditions of the employment and his remuneration. It is conceivable that the mere requirement of six months' notice from a minor performing a menial task would persuade the court that the contract is harsh and oppressive. In that event the contract would not be binding on Jason, and his leaving would not incur him in any liability.

Even if the contract is binding on Jason the remedy available to Simon is somewhat limited. He could not obtain an order which would have the effect of compelling Jason to return to work. The courts have long refused to order specific performance of contracts involving personal service, and such an order is prohibited by s16 Trade Union and Labour Relations Act 1974. Simon would be confined to a claim for damages for the breach of contract and, in view of the nature of the employment and the plaintiff's duty to mitigate his loss, such claim would only realise an extremely modest amount, indeed the damages might only be nominal.

References

1) (1842) 6 M & W 42
2) (1868) LR 4 Ex 32
3) [1908] 2KB 1
4) (1898) 78 LT 296
5) *The Law of Contract* (7th ed) p 427
6) (1800) Peake Add Cas 196
7) (1883) 10 Bing 252
8) (1856) 8 D M & G 254
9) [1894] 2 QB 482
10) [1935] 1 KB 110
11) (1890) 45 Ch D 430